Architectural Design for Tropical Regions

Architectural Design for Tropical Regions

Cleveland Salmon

JOHN WILEY & SONS, INC.

New York • Chichester • Weinheim • Brisbane • Singapore • Toronto

This book is printed on acid-free paper. ⊗

Copyright © 1999 by John Wiley & Sons, Inc. All rights reserved.

Published simultaneously in Canada.

Library of Congress Cataloging-in-Publication Data:
Salmon, Cleveland.
      Architectural design for tropical regions / Cleveland Salmon.
            p.   cm.
      Includes bibliographical references and index.
      ISBN 0-471-18020-3 (cloth : alk. paper)
      1. Architecture, Tropical.   2. Architecture and climate.
I. Title.
NA2542.T7S26   1999
720′.913—dc21   98-38905

Printed in the United States of America.

10 9 8 7 6 5 4 3 2 1

Contents

PART TWO
Climate and Design

Preface

Having experienced the climatic conditions prevalent in tropical regions, and having been exposed to proposals for possible solutions to building problems there, I have developed certain ideas about architectural responses. My thesis study focused on the tropical environment, which made it necessary to develop a great deal of knowledge about the climatic conditions there, as well as the advantages and disadvantages of the solutions presented.

The advantages of this research were threefold. First and foremost, the research supported my thesis study. Second, it added to the knowledge obtained in pursuit of my education.

The third and most significant advantage was the opportunity it gave me to develop and transform my knowledge into its final format, making it available for the many professionals who wish to design effectively while practicing in areas with similar conditions. and to students in pursuit of a degree in architecture.

This book focuses on using the natural environment to produce a comfortable, harmonious, and healthful surrounding. The architecture, culture, and microclimate of the Caribbean, Hawaii, Australia, and Southern California were selected for analysis not just because of the variation in climatic conditions common to all of these areas, but also because of the frequency of seismic and other wind turbulence prevalent there. The design solutions, however, can easily be applied to other tropical regions with similar climatic conditions. These include, but are not limited to, areas with yearly temperature extremes (from highs averaging 97°F and lows of 57°F), average humidity of 56 percent, and wind speed of 16 mph. As a rule, however, each area should be given its own careful analysis, including not

EUROPE

ASIA

AFRICA

AMERICA

SOUTH
PACIFIC

AUSTRALIA

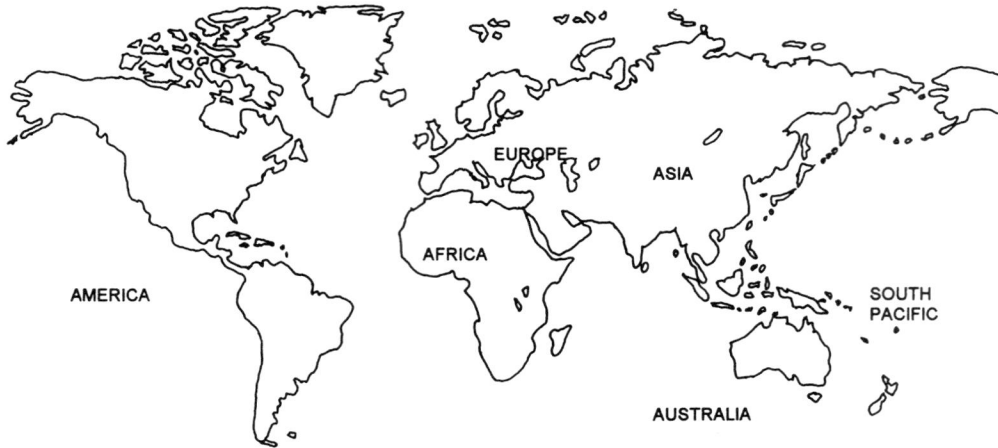

Tropical zones.

only its meteorological data, but also the sunlight, rainfall, landscape, hurricanes, and earthquakes occurring there.

This book includes meteorological data and information on the architecture and culture of tropical regions, an analysis of the influences of each on the built environment, and recommended design concepts and construction techniques as possible approaches to an architectural response. In addition, information is presented to help make economic sense of all the energy-saving devices now available.

Please note that every attempt was made by the author to identify the architect or designer and the date each entry was designed. This information is included with the name of the project, the address, and a brief comment (where applicable). The absence of this information should in no way detract from the importance of each entry and the role of the architect or designer in this area of design.

Acknowledgments

My sincere gratitude to the many individuals and organizations that helped me for their contributions, encouragement, and insights provided during the writing of this book. While it's impossible to name them all, their contribution did not go unnoticed and to them all I am truly greatful.

Special thanks to the staff at the Lila D. Bunch Library, Belmont University, The Jamaica Tourist Board, The LA Conservancy, The Hawaii State Library, and the Library of Congress. I would like to acknowledge my indebtedness to Mr. Lee Askew III, FAIA, for his insights on Australia, for the use of books from his personal library, and for the photographs he provided on Australia. Special thanks also to Prof. Victor Dzidzienyo, Acting Dean of the School of Architecture and Planning, Howard University, and Mr. Hans Hesse, architect, for their comments and guidance; their contributions had great influence on the book's final form. To Mr. Dryck Roberts, historian and Chairman of the Spanish Town Historic Foundation, I extend my thanks for sharing his knowledge and providing guidance.

Last but not least, my sincere thanks to all those who facilitated my field trips and allowed me to photograph their houses and places of business, often without prior notice.

Cleveland Salmon, AIA

Introduction

Our ability to work efficiently, and indeed our very survival, depend on our environment. The ability to integrate our needs with the forces acting on our environment makes our daily routine simpler and more in tune with the natural elements of our climate.

The tropical marine climate is one of the most comfortable and enjoyable in the world. However, the ability to respond to the demands of the microclimate, and not in spite of it, is the key to optimizing its potential. At any given time, the forces acting on any area will determine the type of mammal, bird, insect, fish, or vegetable life that is likely to survive according to how well they adapt to each element. Landscape and climate thus dictate the general rules for a comfortable existence, and the ability to balance or use just enough of each element to encourage proper regeneration is the key to long-range survival.

The tropical climate has four main components: (1) temperature, (2) humidity, (3) wind, and (4) sunlight. Other elements affecting the built environment that should also be considered are the effect of (5) precipitation and, of course, (6) landscape characteristics, which have a marked effect on our exposure to any of the first four elements. The unique features of soil, weather, and terrain are some of the key factors determining the different approaches to an architectural problem.

In creating the built environment, the architect is influenced not only by the microclimate, but also by the work of others and by other influences that make up his or her culture. Therefore, it is essential for the architect to understand not just the climate, but also the culture of the people of the tropics when creating an environment for them. The architect should also take into account not only the client's immediate expressed needs, but also his or her desires, which may result from the client's position in society, and may allow him or her to adjust to the influences of the modern world and the differences which they are willing to embrace.

The three main considerations influencing architectural design in the tropics can be summarized as (1) people and their needs, (2) climate and its effect, and (3) materials and construction techniques.

PEOPLE AND THEIR NEEDS

Individuals generally respond differently from social groups, and the circumstances of their gathering and their surrounding play a vital role in influencing their response. While it is difficult to understand all the influences on a client's expressed needs, the architect, by training, can interpret them accurately and, through familiarity and imagination, create buildings that reflect these needs.

The manufacturing potential of the industrial age has brought about significant changes, especially in agriculture, where machine replacement of human labor (a way of life and a source of income) is one of the dominant phenomena of tropical life, and one very difficult to accept. New goods bring new desires, roadside stalls are replaced with strip malls, and movie theaters and television bring images of modern cities. The architect thus has the special task of providing buildings and towns that allow their inhabitants to accommodate the complex mechanisms of modern life without sacrificing freedom and dignity.

Development brings with it modification and sometimes the destruction of habits and customs stretching back many generations and often interwoven with religious beliefs. In most cases, traders, missionaries, government, and television have exerted strong influence (good or bad), and it is often left up to the architect and planner to remedy past mistakes and safeguard the future. Many changes have been accepted by the people of the tropics, who are willing and even anxious to share in what they perceive as the modern benefits of Western civilization and culture. Past experience has provided us with an understanding of the use of industrialism. We are therefore able to recognize its potential pitfalls and to work out satisfactory responses that blend the social and industrial elements to provide a comfortable and attractive life for all classes of people in these regions.

CLIMATE AND ITS EFFECTS

Sunshine and an even distribution of rainfall on a tropical island brings to life an abundance of vegetation and insect life that support a varied animal world. Two distinct environments are produced. In one, air temperature equals or is slightly below body temperature. In the other, air temperature is near or above body temperature. Here, under low cloud cover, the saturated air does very little to evaporate sweat and cool the skin.

In the first environment, mere shielding from the rain and cold will suffice. In the second, the dwelling must block the rain and sun but also cool the body with breezes, either natural or artificial. The sun raises the temperature, but the saturated air prevents the perspiration that allows the body to adjust normally. In the hot-wet tropics, buildings should shun the hot, dust-laiden air while taking advantage of the cooling effect of breezes. The tempo of life is much slower in the hot-wet tropics because of the humidity associated with the low cloud cover and hot, moist air. Seasons vary as the clouds roll back for long periods, bringing short droughts and intense sunshine. For the most part, clouds and sun alternate, and neither day nor night brings much alteration in the humidity level.

MATERIALS AND CONSTRUCTION TECHNIQUES

Buildings are permanent in intent, and the builder needs to weigh the long-term future against the present cost. Building materials, if not readily available locally, may need to be imported or manufactured if necessary. The country's productive possibilities and material resources should all be examined, and adjustments made to manage the construction process and maintain control in all circumstances.

The tropical climate produces conditions that affect both people and their buildings. Large daily temperature ranges stress building materials when dry, and even more severely during the seasonal rains, which, though short, can be heavy.

The design process involves thousands of decisions and choices in order to satisfy the various needs of society. First, there is the social need for which the building is designed. Here, since a building will last indefinitely, the future trends of society must be weighed against its present demand and its course thereby changed for good or ill. The tropical marine climate presents the architect with a palette of design elements; giving the right response to the climate and setting, is aesthetically pleasing and adds beauty to the end result. The architect's responsibility to the culture and the climate ensures sensitivity to social and environmental issues and also provides the basis for excellence in the design solution.

PART ONE

Regional Profiles

1

The Caribbean

INTRODUCTION

The Caribbean islands stretch nearly 1,900 miles from Barbados to the eastern tip of Cuba. Except for Jamaica and the Cayman Islands, they form a 1,000-mile curving archipelago stretching from the Bahamas in the north to Trinidad in the south. We do not have the space to deal with all the islands, each worthy of its own treatment, but we shall describe Jamaica in detail and in the process observe many diverse civilizations dominated by a wide variety of European nations—Spain, England, France—and societies unrelated to Europe: Tainos (Arawaks), African, Chinese, and East Indians. The resulting population and culture are a fusion of these ethnic traditions, the mix being evident in Jamaica's homegrown cuisine, art, entertainment, and architecture.

The island's history is rooted in the sugar plantation economy, and the slave era still weighs heavy on the national psyche. Its rich heritage reaches back to pre-Columbian days when the Amerindians etched petroglyphs on the ceilings and walls of caverns. Examples

The Caribbean region.

can still be seen in caves throughout the island. Christopher Columbus first landed on Jamaica in 1494 and found perhaps 100,000 Tainos (Arawak Amerindians), who had settled Jamaica around 700 A.D. Columbus described Jamaica as the "fairest isle that eye behold; mountainous all full of valleys and fields and plains."

The island's climate, especially its temperature, rainfall, and local winds, is considerably influenced by topography. Although Jamaica is relatively small, it has much elevated land that rises gradually from all sides. The highest point, for example, is the Blue Mountain in eastern Jamaica, which rises to 7,360 feet. This unique feature varies the temperature of the island and requires special considerations in temperature modification to maintain comfort.

ARCHITECTURE AND CULTURE

Tainos

The Taino Amerindians living in Jamaica and other islands were one of the most peaceful people in the world. They were the first of the two major tribes inhabiting the Caribbean and were part of a much wider migration that had its origins not in America, but in Asia.

The North American Continent was populated over 27,000 years ago by Palaeo Indians who crossed from Siberia by a land bridge and slowly dispersed into Central America. The pedestrian explorers following herds of bison and caribou from the Pacific fringes of Siberia, reached Tlapacoya in Mexico 23,000 years ago and had drifted into the highlands of South America 3,000 years after this.

(Duly, p. 53)

The Tainos inhabited the Caribbean for over 1,400 years, with traces found around the River Orinoco in South America dating back almost 2,000 years. They were not a single people living in one place, like the Maya, Aztec, or Inca, but a group of peoples with a common Arawakian language. When they migrated north from South America, they settled in groups in the various Caribbean islands. The first Jamaicans were part of this vast migration. They named the island they discovered Xaymaca, which means "land of wood and water." There were splendid forests that they could use for foraging and retreat. They obtained food from fish and shellfish, and although there is no trace of the original Amerindian house, one would assume that wood and other tree products were the original materials for buildings in Jamaica. Some of the houses were very large, like those in Trinidad, which were bell-shaped, and housed about 100 people. The houses in Jamaica were simple thatched roofs on wood posts, clear underneath or with a room inside. Sometimes the low roof overhang was joined to the ground by a thatched wall. When this happened, windows and doors could be inserted. It is possible that these walls were made from bamboo, branches, or roseau woven between larger uprights. The spaces between the weave were finished off with

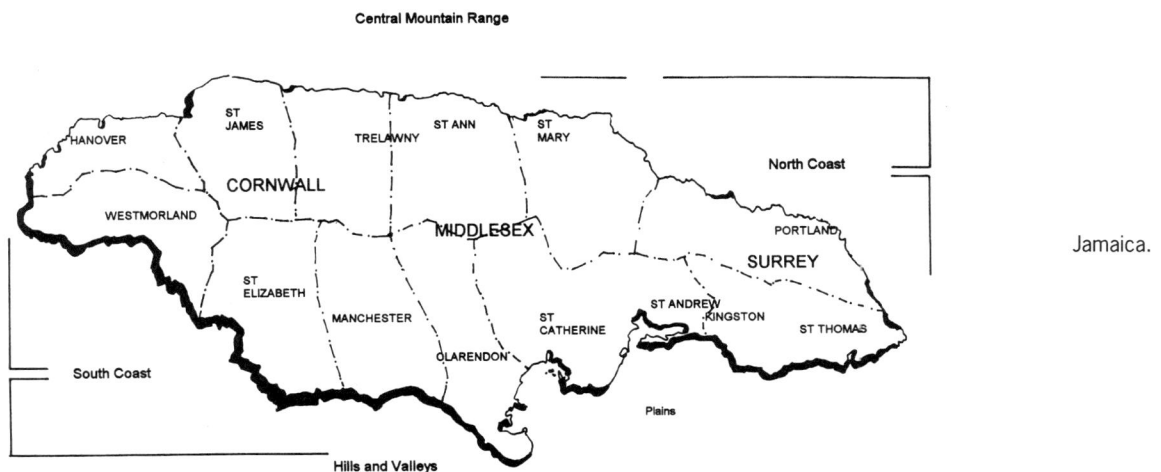

Jamaica.

Bell-shaped Huts, Trinidad and other islands of the Lesser Antilles.

THE HUTS DESCRIBED BY LAS CASAS WERE IN THE SHAPE OF BELLS (F. M. PADRON) BUILT BY AMERINDIANS IN TRINIDAD AND OTHER ISLANDS OF THE LESSER ANTILLES

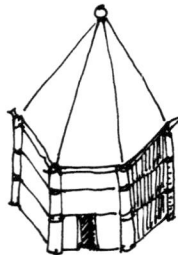

Taino dwelling in Jamaica.

FAMILY HUTS CONSISTED OF A TALL CENTER POLE SURROUNDED BY AN ARRANGMENT OF SHORTER POSTS, FITTED WITH CANES AND VINES; USED TO FORM THE WALLS. THE CACIQUE'S HUT WAS DIFFERENT IN THAT IT WAS OF A RECTANGULAR SHAPE

Cacique's hut.

a clay mixture to form the exterior walls. We assume that there were cocorite forests (under stable wet conditions, as there are now) to supply the thatch for the roof. The cacique's (leader's) house was often larger than the ordinary houses and was rectangular in shape.

The Tainos were the first great architects of Jamaica. The houses, called "tapia," and ceremonial dwellings that Columbus saw were whatever size the tribe desired. Their houses evolved into a vernacular form that was the purest expression of Jamaican architecture. The prototype was a system rather than a form, as many versions were possible, and it was based on suitability for the climate, convenience, economy, and comfort. The Jamaican Tainos dwellings were generally situated on a rise in clearings near the sea, with a view southward. Tree-covered hills were behind them. The weaving, the joining, and the spacing of the uprights created design and patterning. The houses the Tainos built were cool, rainproof, and windproof, and needed only slight repairs if they were well built.

Elsewhere in the Caribbean, Jean Baptiste Labat, the French Jesuit priest, in his writings referred to the natives as "Caraibes" and their dwelling as "Carbets." According to Hulme and Whitehead, Labat "arrived in the French Antilles in 1694 and returned to France in 1705. He administered over both Guadeloupe and Martinique, becoming Superior of the Guadeloupe mission in 1702, and Procurator of Martinique, for the second time, in 1703."

> The houses of the Caraibes are called Carbets. I know nothing of the etymology of this name. I have never heard it said that there was any other in the whole of Martinique than that of La Rose. This Carbet was around sixty feet long, by twenty-four to twenty-five feet wide; it was made a little bit like a market-hall. The small posts rose nine feet off the ground, & the large ones in proportion. The rafters touched the ground on both sides, the lathes were of reeds, and the roofing, which was of palm leaves also came down below the rafters. One of the ends of the Carbet was completely closed off with reeds, & covered with palm leaves, reserving one opening for going into the kitchen. The other end was almost all open.
>
> (Hulme and Whitehead, p. 156)

Whether the Amerindians in this region called their dwellings Carbets is still debatable. The French derivation is probably from nautical usage since "Carbet" is a ship's large cabin. Despite the language barrier, one can assume that whatever the natives called their dwellings, if accurately recorded, sounds similar, if not identical, to "Carbet." In any event, the prototype described by the various colonists in their many writings is similar in many respects and has

Taino's hammock. (From Fred Olsen, described in *On the Trail of the Arawaks,* University of Oklahoma Press, 1975, pp. 221 and 359.)

evolved over the centuries to a true form of architectural expression worthy of a second look.

The Spaniards

On May 5, 1494, Christopher Columbus landed at Maima and became the first European to set foot on Jamaican soil. Maima was one of the largest towns established by the Tainos. There they fashioned their canoes, built their houses, and fished in the rivers and the Caribbean Sea. Columbus lived in Maima, which he named Sevilla la Nueva (New Seville), for over 1 year. Spanish records and excavations at Sevilla la Nueva revealed that the first houses were built of wood and bamboo, mud and thatch modeled after the Amerindian dwelling.

Spanish settlers arrived beginning in 1510, raising cattle and pigs and introducing sugar and slavery, which would profoundly shape the islands' future. By the end of the 16th century the Taino population had been entirely wiped out as a result of hard labor, ill treatment, and European diseases to which they had no resistance. However, while the natives and their village life did not survive, their building technology did as the Spanish adopted the native tradition of building to set up their settlements.

Spanish Town, founded in 1534, is the oldest continuously occupied city in the Western Hemisphere. It became the capital of Jamaica when the Spaniards abandoned Sevilla la Nueva on the inhospitable north coast and moved to the fat, fertile plains of the south. They called the new town St. Jago de la Vega. Today the Spanish period is

View of Nueva Sevilla from the Seville Estate Seville Coastline St. Ann, Jamaica

The Seville Estate overlooks the Seville coastal plain, site of one of the oldest pre-Columbian cities in the Western Hemisphere and the site of Columbus's one-year stay in Jamaica.

recalled in street names: White Church Street, where they built the Church of the White Cross; Red Church Street, where they built the Church of the Red Cross; and Monk Street, where there was a monastery. In 1640 a British buccaneer who plundered the Spanish settlement described it as a fair town consisting of 400 or 500 houses built mostly with canes overcast with mortar. The town had five or six stately churches and chapels and one Franciscan monastery.

The Spanish made no attempt to build in the classical mode in the 17th century in the Caribbean or indeed in any of the later styles. Walling, a technique attributed to the Spanish, used a timber frame with stone and mortar filling was used in Seville la Nueva. This technique has survived the period of British occupation and is still used today to build houses in Jamaica. Apart from the walling system, the Spanish left very little of their heritage in the Caribbean. Those living in Spanish Town, Jamaica, as well as in St. Joseph, Trinidad, used the Amerindian technique of building. In 1612, Trinidad's then Governor Sancho de Alguiza told the king of Spain:

I spent 16 days on the voyage and arrived on the 29th December at the Island at which there is a town called San Joseph de Oruna containing as many as thirty-two straw huts and about 40 men.

(Sancho de Alquiza to the King of Spain,
14th June 1616. British museum)

Communicating with the Dutch West Indian Company in 1637, San Joseph, then Secretary to Tobago, wrote:

The houses are made of earth stamped solid which they call tapias and roofed with thatched or other combustible material. Almost in the center of the town stands the church in which the Spaniards keep a watch of 5–6 men, day and night.

(A Report by Ousiel, Secretary of Tobago to the
Dutch West India Company, December 1637.)

The houses occupied by early settlers on the other islands were similar to the Amerindian's dwellings in both their use of materials and design. In his report to Lord Macartney in 1777, Phillipe Roume de St. Laurent described the houses in Port of Spain, Trinidad, as follows:

At the first coming of the foreign nations into the Islands they lodged much after the same manner as the natural inhabitants of the country, in little cots and huts made of the wood they felled upon the place as they cleared the ground. There are many still to be seen in several of the newly-planted colonies, many of these weak structures which are sustained only by four or six forks planted in the ground and, instead of walls, are encompassed and palizaded only with reeds and covered with palm or plantain leaves, sugar canes or some such materials.

A Report to Lord Macartney, Governor of Grenada, by
P.R. Roume de St. Laurent of his visit to Trinidad 1777,
Public Record Office, State Papers, Colonial C.O. 101/2.

The Spaniards' grafting of the Amerindian prototype onto their own construction is well documented and is a testament to the appropriateness of the building type to the region. That the Spaniards, with all their culture, could not or would not impose their own historical heritage on the region is also a triumph for the Amerindians. The Amerindian house is obviously economical, rapidly built, cheap, and comfortable.

The British

In 1655 a British expedition landed a few miles south of Passage Fort, Jamaica, and proceeded to capture the city and the island, with very little resistance from the Spaniards, who packed up their valuables and sailed to Cuba. In a short time, all the adobe buildings they left behind in Spanish Town had been destroyed or replaced. The Cathedral Church of St. James, built on the ruins of the Spanish Church of the Red Cross, on Red Church Street, was one of the first Anglican Cathedrals built outside of England. This cathedral was destroyed by a hurricane in 1712 and rebuilt in 1714. In 1843 it was named the Cathedral of the Jamaica Diocese of the Anglican Church. Despite ongoing efforts of the Spanish loyalists and guerrilla-style campaigns of freed Spanish slaves (Cimarrones or Maroons), England took control of the island. The profits accrued from cocoa, coffee, and sugarcane production hastened further settlement. But with Britain constantly at war with France or Spain, effective control of the island was entrusted to buccaneers, a band of political refugees and escaped criminals, who committed themselves to lives of piracy against the Spaniards. Depending on whether Britain and Spain had just signed or just broken peace agreements, Britain either supported the buccaneers or helped Spain repel them.

Jamaica's British colonial history began in the mid-1600s and ended with the Declaration of Independence in 1962. It lasted for more than 300 years, enough time for seven generations to be born. During that time the New World changed enormously. The colonists brought their traditions from England, including those governing how they lived, worked, and worshiped. They also re-created, as much as possible, their traditional ways of building houses, barns, and fences. Shelter was the immediate need. At first, the buccaneers occupied the dwellings left behind by the Spanish when the island was captured. As more settlers arrived, they built modest cottages, as they did back home, as this was the quickest, most practical way to establish themselves and provide for their needs. The timber-framed houses built in Spanish Town and elsewhere in the first century of settlement were essentially English in

Cathedral of the Jamaica Diocese of the Anglican Church Spanish Town, Jamaica

The Cathedral Church of St. James, on Red Church Street, was the first Anglican cathedral outside of England. It was built on the ruins of the Spanish Church of the Red Cross, which was razed by Cromwell's soldiers.

appearance. The furniture they made looked English because the new settlers had come primarily from England. With the passage of time and the establishment of prosperous households, settlers in Jamaican colonies quickly revealed their desire for style. What was fashionable in Europe, however, generally did not appear in the colonies until a decade or two later.

Seventeenth-century rooms had low ceilings and were dimly lit by small casement windows. The timber framing was exposed and usually whitewashed. Building styles linked the Old World to the New. Most of the houses built in Jamaica in the first century of settlement closely resembled those in England, but using Jamaican materials and modified to provide shade from the afternoon sun. The settlers raised structures with massive timber frames to meet their basic needs then filled in the walls with wattle and daub. These houses were added to throughout the century. Early in the 1700s, new architectural influences were introduced. Façades became more important; the exterior became an integrated and logical design, balanced and symmetrical. By the middle of the 18th century, fashion-

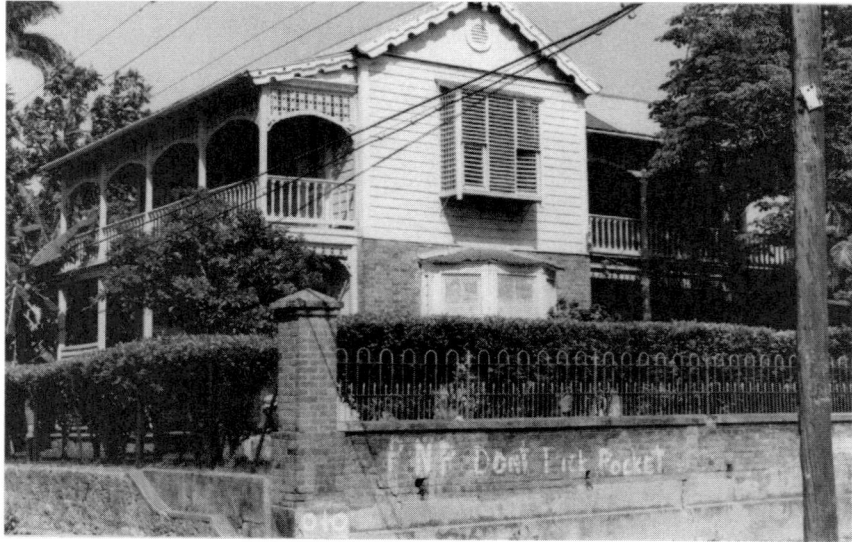

Colonial House
White Church Street
Spanish Town, Jamaica

able houses were being built in the Georgian style (named for the English monarchs who reigned at the time). Interiors were characterized by bigger rooms and larger windows.

A distinctively Jamaican colonial style of building developed as the colonies matured and as the settlers adapted to their new environment. In the 17th century, the main difference between English and Jamaican styles was the degree of simplification, in part because of the very small number of highly skilled craftsmen among the earliest settlers. The early dwellings of the colonies varied widely from

Buxton House   1911
Mico College Campus,
14 Marescaux Road
Kingston, Jamaica

A colonial-style building currently owned by Mico College Trustee and The government of Jamaica.

elegant plantation mansions to one-room houses. The typical house of the dirt farmer was dark and drafty and had a dirt floor. Scattered throughout the island were large plantation houses modeled on the vast country houses of England.

Caribbean Timber House of Freed African Slaves

Slave rebellions didn't make life easy for the English as escaped slaves joined with descendants of freed Spanish slaves, the Maroons, engaging in extended guerilla-style campaigns and eventually forcing the English to grant them autonomy in 1739. New slaves kept arriving, however, most of them put to work on sugar plantations under appalling conditions. Slaves were burned, strangled, and otherwise tortured to terrorize them into obedience. There were constant insurrections, especially after the American War of Independence (1775–81) and the French Revolution (1789), which were all squashed with the utmost severity. The Jamaica Parliament finally abolished slavery on August 1, 1834.

The houses developed by the freed Africans had a very close relationship with nature, weathering quickly and needing renewal but protected by the shade of nearby fruit trees that provided a natural setting not possible on other arid islands. The English influence was predominant and was quickly standardized due to hurricanes and fires. The builders used Amerindian techniques for walls and roofs, but with increasing prefabrication of structural supports using pre-sawn timber. The houses were paneled in clapboard similar to the vendor stall structures frequently seen on rural streets.

The African Slave Settlement 1690–1840 Seville Estate St. Ann, Jamaica

The settlement developed in two stages. Stage one (1690–1750) consisted of two rows of houses close together and to the west of the Great House. The second stage (1750–1840) developed to the north of the first, with more space between each house. Houses were constructed using the Amerindian roof system of wattle-and-daub walls.

The African hillside wattle-and-daub houses differed from the Amerindian dwelling, as the floor system was raised off the ground rather than being on the ground. This was necessary to allow for beam depth underneath and for ventilation, as well as to compensate for the unevenness of the ground. The house frame was built on "pillar trees" (stub columns or piers) placed at the corners and in the middle to fit the spans. The roof, however, remained clearly a part of the Amerindian heritage. The house itself consisted of bamboo walls woven horizontally between wood uprights set between the main posts, which were placed at 3- to 4-foot centers. Wattle-and-daub, a combination of clay earth mixed with grasses and saplings as a binder, was applied to the open-weave wall to seal it. Originally made of round wood logs, small saplings, and, later, sawn logs, the house was completely framed in wood. The roof was rethatched after the first rainy season. Small wood shutters closed the window openings. Sometimes the walls were a mixture of cement, sand, and bagasse. (Bagasse is the dry crushed end product of sugar cane.) This is undoubtedly the quickest, most economical means of constructing a dwelling. It was a perfect solution and the most suitable architectural response to the need for housing. The demands of cooking and toileting were dealt with outside, far from the house. Later, the use of kerosene allowed the kitchen to be incorporated into the house or attached to one side.

Public Buildings

Under the Spanish, clay, wood, and thatch were used for both public and domestic building. The English demonstrated their political

**House of Assembly
Spanish Town Square
Spanish Town, Jamaica**

strength on Jamaica by erecting public buildings, something the Spanish never achieved. This is clearly demonstrated in the church architecture of the 19th century. One of the principal 19th-century building systems was a combination of brick and stone. The bricks were imported from England as ballast. The openings, doorways, and keyed corners were built first. The openings were framed up, which established the jambs. The load was distributed over the openings by means of a shallow brick arch. The bricks permitted accurate dimensions, as they were standard prefabricated units all the same size. In some instances, the walls were pointed in lime mortar and then plastered and rendered. This process covered the whole wall, hiding the brick and stone keyed joints. This method of building in Jamaica has almost disappeared. The remaining examples are found only in church façades and in a few public buildings like the original Kings House, (1762), the Old Court House, and the Assembly Building (1762) in

Rodney Memorial   1762
Spanish Town Square
Spanish Town, Jamaica

Old Kings House   1762
Spanish Town Square
Spanish Town, Jamaica

Ward Theater   1907
North Parade
Kingston, Jamaica

North of Parade, the Ward theater was built after the 1907 earthquake on the site of the municipal Theater Royal. The magnificent theater was recently refurbished, complementing its excellent acoustics.

Spanish Town. The Spanish Town square, which was completed 1819, is one of the best examples of a Georgian square outside of Britain.

The Estate House

The "great houses" were developed by the British sugarcane farmers who lived on the plains to suit their particular circumstances. The indentured laborers and freed slaves who worked the cane fields built hillside wattle-and-daub houses, and the English descendants of the colonists who triumphed at the end of the 1800s created sugar estates and erected mansions.

The estate houses began as rural two-storied timber cottages, most of which have long since disappeared. Estates were divided into series of quarters graded according to rank. The workers lived in a room with a

Kingston Parish Church
South Parade
Kingston, Jamaica

Kingston Parish Church, south of Parade, was destroyed by the 1907 earthquake and rebuilt. The clock tower was erected as a memorial to those killed in the First World War. The bell dates back to 1715.

**Seville Great House
1745
Seville Estate
St. Ann, Jamaica**

The house was originally a two-story structure constructed primarily of wattle and daub, with a shingle roof. The verandah, which was added later, is partially surrounded by a louvered wall for screening and natural ventilation.

Dutch, or barn, door—the top and bottom halves of the door being hinged separately. Their barracks were a series of such rooms joined together and nicknamed "jackass barracks." There were also quarters and sometimes houses for the overseer and supervisors. As the estate grew, so did the size and decoration of the estate houses. The later houses were magnificent, feminine and monumental. The great house, where the master lived, dominated the site, with its formal garden, decorated fretwork, and crystal chandelier.

**Seville Great House
1745
Seville Estate
St. Ann, Jamaica**

**Craighton House   1805
Newcastle Road
St. Andrew, Jamaica**

The original house, named after its first owner, George Craighton, was built in or around 1805. Located 2,600 feet above sea level, it is a very attractive colonial house with a large, flat plateau of lawn at the front and a commanding view to the east and west.

The location and splendor of the estate house played a big part in the dominance of the plantation owner over his subjects. He lived in great splendor, entertained on a grand scale, and provided a welcome to wearily travelers after their long journey. His large house, typically of eight to ten rooms, was spacious, with high ceilings that kept the building cool. The house usually sat back from the entry gate, with ample grounds in front for formal gardens. Behind the main building were many rooms to house the servants, as well as the kitchen and bathrooms.

**Devon House   1881
Corner of Waterloo Road
and Hope Road
Kingston, Jamaica**

Devon House is the most elegant surviving 19th-century mansion. The house was built in 1881 by George Steibel, a black shipwright's apprentice and builder's foreman. The Georgian-style architecture was adapted to tropical conditions, with wide louvered windows, deep patios, and wide over-hangs.

Devon House   1881
Corner of Waterloo and
Hope Road
Kingston, Jamaica

View along the verandah.

Developments of the 20th Century

The Taino house plan crafted by the Amerindians and developed by the Spanish and British, was later transformed by the standardization of its parts through American technology. At the end of the 19th century another transformation occurred, but this time it was more gradual, taking almost fifty years to complete. During this period, wood slowly gave way to concrete and clay products. This period can also

House
18 Montclaire Drive
Beverly Hills
St. Andrew, Jamaica

House
5¼ Weyclift Close
Beverly Hills
St. Andrew, Jamaica

be viewed as the one in which both wood and concrete were used in
the same building. The adaptation of concrete, concrete products,
and clay blocks into building components changed the form of house
construction. Although concrete was rigid (providing structural stability and durability), its rendering or cement plaster was subject to
cracking. The timber houses, on the other hand, blended well with
their surroundings, swaying and bending with the wind while sitting
lightly on their supports. Yards were planted with ground produce,

Matalon House
Beverly Hills
St. Andrew, Jamaica

Department of Psychiatry
University of the West Indies
Mona Campus
St. Andrew, Jamaica

Mutual Life Center
1 Oxford Road
Kingston, Jamaica

Cable and Wireless
11 Carlton Crescent
New Kingston, Jamaica

with fruit trees and other trees providing shade from the intense heat of the sun.

Independence created an expanded middle class in the 1960s and 1970s, with dwellings today approaching mansions perched atop Beverly Hills, Red Hills, and Skyline Drive in Upper St. Andrew and elsewhere on the island. This new expression of Jamaican architecture in concrete, and concrete blocks and mortar, was heavily influenced by American styles and inspired by migration of Jamaicans to Miami, only 45 minutes by air to the west. Living standards rose, and washing machines and deep freezers became popular. Thin beams, projecting beyond the eaves, creating patios and carports, were decorated with elaborate grillwork and miniature Doric and Ionic columns cast in concrete. Polished terrazzo floors, burglar bars, venetian blinds, and eventually carpet in place of vinyl tiles became essential in the 1970s. As air conditioners became popular, more people began demanding them to cool their homes, especially in the late evenings and at night. The main bedrooms were the first space to turn away from natural venting and isolate itself from the outside world. This isolation increased as other bedrooms were closed up and then the entire house. Central air conditioning provided the environment, and television provided the scenery.

Before long, it also became necessary for middle-class families to further isolate and protect themselves from their neighbors and from the fast-growing ghetto areas below the hills. However, while this was the trend, it was by no means general; the majority of the citizens of Jamaica continued to enjoy their surroundings. This is a clear indication of how architecture can and does influence our lives. Our progress in technology has created materials that, if not utilized effectively, can make our lives worse than before.

Using concrete blocks as walls meant that the walls gained weight and required stiffening and sometimes bracing. With stick frame construction, the same framing can be used for walls and for supporting the floors and the roof. But concrete or clay blocks are made only for stacking vertically in compression. In addition, the height of all the walls should be the same to facilitate placement of the reinforced concrete belt beam sitting on top, joining all the walls together. This arrangement stabilizes the walls, acts as a lintel over the doors and windows, and receives the wall plate to take the rafters.

New emphasis on the solid wall diminished the importance of the roof as a design feature. The gabled roof slowly gave way to lower (almost flat) reinforced concrete slabs in the late 1930s. This roof system continued to dominate the domestic dwelling market after

**House
50 Palmoral Ave
Mona Heights
St. Andrew, Jamaica**

1945 and covered a multitude of house plans in most of the housing schemes in Kingston.

During the 1980s, the one-way pitch gave way to a shallow two-way roof, which is sometimes combined with a flat slab over carports, verandahs, and entrances. The attempt to create a balance is an ongoing process, but it does appear that the traditional mode of building is returning. The traditional architectural style of Jamaica,

**House
12 Liguanea Terrace
St. Andrew, Jamaica**

House
10 Liguanea Terrace
St. Andrew, Jamaica

and indeed of the entire Caribbean, can be described as some version of the Tainos hillside tapia, with a roof of more than one pitch and with wood being the leading building material, utilizing colored or split-faced concrete blocks, decorative blocks for ventilation, wood casements, and three light windows with wood louvers. The heritage of Jamaican architecture, as we have seen, involves biodegradable materials that eventually decay. While it is not economically feasible to live as the Tainos did, their building style is worth revisiting as a concept to be improved on.

CLIMATIC DATA

The climate of the Caribbean region throughout the year is largely under the influence of the northeast trade winds. They blow steadily across the tropical waters south of east from May to November and north of east the remainder of the year. There is very little difference in the uniform regularity of the climate pattern in the maritime areas and over land. Disturbances in the warm blanket of air occur only at intervals when there is an invasion of cold continental air from the North American continent or when a tropical cyclone is forming in the Caribbean Sea. Because of the rugged mountainous terrain of the islands, thunderstorms are often frequent, more so over land than over the sea. The temperature decreases rather rapidly with elevation, but the extremes, such as occasional freezing temperatures found in high interior valleys, are the result of the invasion of cold continental air from the north, with the typography exerting only a secondary influence.

Temperature

At sea level the mean annual temperature, as represented by the records at Kingston, Morant Point, and Negril Point, Jamaica, is about 79°F. (26°C). The coolest month is February (76°F), (24°C) and the warmest is August (82°F). (28°C). The temperature can be above 90°F (32°C) in all months, although this is uncommon in winter and early spring (December, January, February, and March). The highest temperature of record at Kingston is 97°F (36°C) in August.

In winter (December, January, and February) the temperature does not often fall as low as 65°F. (18°C). The usual low temperature at night in summer (June, July, and August) is between 70° and 76°F. (21° and 24°C). At Kingston the lowest temperature of record is 57°F in each of the winter months.

At higher elevations it is much cooler. At Hill Gardens (about 5,000 feet above sea level) the mean annual temperature is 62°F. (17°C). It is therefore important for architects to be knowledgable about the climate and the different design responses required; sometimes, in extreme cases, heating is needed to maintain comfort. A normally tolerable average temperature range is between 60° and 80°F. (16° and 27°C). If the average temperature falls below or above this range, cooling or heating is general desired.

Average Temperature—Kingston, Jamaica

	JAN	FEB	MAR	APR	MAY	JUN	JUL	AUG	SEP	OCT	NOV	DEC
(C)	26.6	26.4	26.9	27.5	28.3	29.1	29.1	29.1	28.9	28.6	27.7	27.2
(F)	80.0	79.5	80.5	81.5	83.0	84.5	84.5	84.5	84.0	83.5	82.0	81.0

Humidity

Humidity is water moisture suspended in air and is measured as the percentage of the air saturated by water. At 100 percent relative humidity for a given temperature, the air cannot accept or hold additional moisture.

Microclimate comfort is directly influenced by humidity. A comfortable relative humidity range is generally between 20 percent and 60 percent. For example, at 77°F with little air motion, the range of relative humidity for interior comfort would be between 20 percent and 50 percent.

The relative humidity at Kingston, Jamaica, is high, averaging about 75 percent year round. It ranges between 75 percent and 80 percent in autumn and early winter. Combined with the high temperature, this high humidity creates an oppressive condition when wind movement is light.

Wind

In no months are there any southerly components of the wind over the open Caribbean Sea. The average wind speed is generally low, with relatively little deviation from the mean.

The Caribbean islands lie in an area where the prevailing winds (trades) are northeast to east throughout the year, but with frequent southeast winds in summer and autumn. Along the shores of the islands there are distinct diurnal variations. At Kingston, Jamaica, the winds are about equally divided between southeasterly and north-northeasterly. The wind is strongest in early afternoon (6 to 8 knots) and weakest just before sunrise (about 2 knots).

Rainfall

The amount of precipitation in the form of rain, hail, or dew, which delivers water to the land, does much to determine the microclimate. Annual rainfall varies significantly from coastal mountains to coastal plains. This naturally affects the amount and type of plant growth. As indicated in the rainfall table for Kingston, Jamaica receives more rain per month from May to December, a period that also has the warmest temperatures for the year. More rain is also recorded inland and over the mountainous area of the island than over coastal low-lying areas.

Rainfall is relatively light in the lee of the mountains but abundant elsewhere. On the windward slopes of the mountains, rains are frequently heavy to torrential. The winter and early spring months, as a rule, have less rain. There is diminished rain in midsummer. Wet periods come in May and June and again in autumn. Some heavy rains of the latter season accompany tropical storms.

Average Rainfall—Kingston, Jamaica

	JAN	FEB	MAR	APR	MAY	JUN	JUL	AUG	SEP	OCT	NOV	DEC
(mm)	30.1	22.9	38.1	38.1	104.1	96.5	45.7	106.7	127.0	172.7	96.5	40.6
(in.)	1.2	0.9	0.9	1.5	4.1	3.8	1.8	4.2	5.0	6.8	3.8	1.6

Hurricanes

Normally in tropical and subtropical regions frequented by West Indian hurricanes, the weather from day to day shows little variation.

PREVAILING WINDS MOVE WITH THE ARROW'S
DIRECTION AND FREQUENCY:

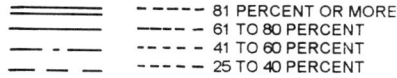

======== - - - - - 81 PERCENT OR MORE
———————— - - - - 61 TO 80 PERCENT
— - — - — - - - - 41 TO 60 PERCENT
— — — - - - - 25 TO 40 PERCENT

AVERAGE VELOCITY:

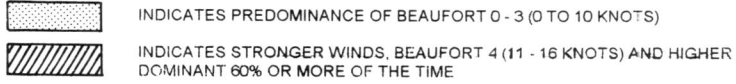

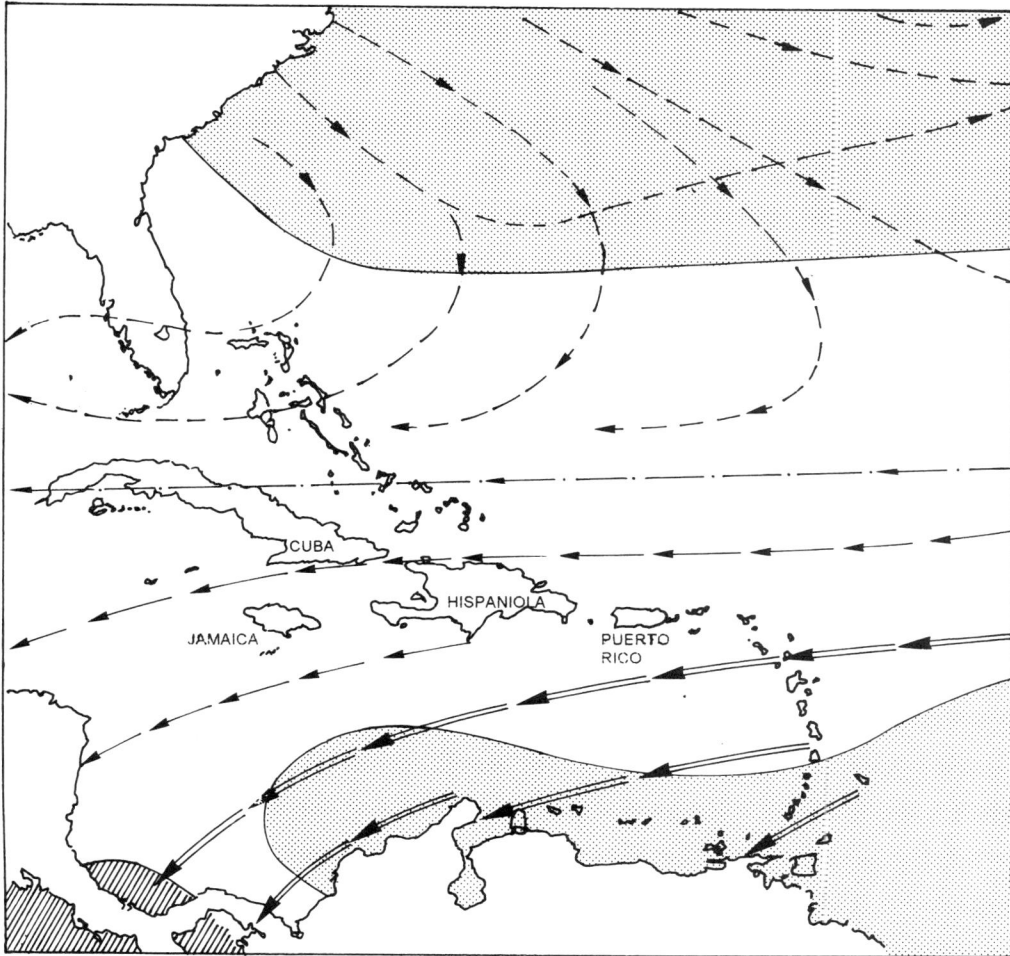

INDICATES PREDOMINANCE OF BEAUFORT 0 - 3 (0 TO 10 KNOTS)

INDICATES STRONGER WINDS, BEAUFORT 4 (11 - 16 KNOTS) AND HIGHER
DOMINANT 60% OR MORE OF THE TIME

Predominant ocean winds.

With even the slightest departure in the stability of prevailing
weather conditions, the formation of a hurricane can be suspected
while it is still many miles away. One of the first signs is the sea
swell—long, unbroken waves at sea formed by the circulatory hurricane winds and advancing far ahead of the storm.

There are two principal places of origin of West Indian hurricanes—the west Caribbean Sea and the Atlantic Ocean just south of the Cape Verde Islands. Occasionally, they also develop in other parts of the West Indian region, though not all of them can be traced to the point of genesis.

Hurricanes of the western Caribbean sometimes develop in May. In June they are somewhat more common, usually moving toward the west, northwest, or north. They rarely form in the western Caribbean Sea in July or August, but by the end of September they occasionally are found there. Some form there in November. On average, the July hurricanes are somewhat intense, reaching major intensity in August.

Data gathered after hurricanes show that they are phenomena of primary importance. Loads caused by hurricanes on buildings and other structures are not secondary loads, and although equivalent static loads are generally used for wind design, the turbulence and

Track and wind system of a West Indian hurricane.

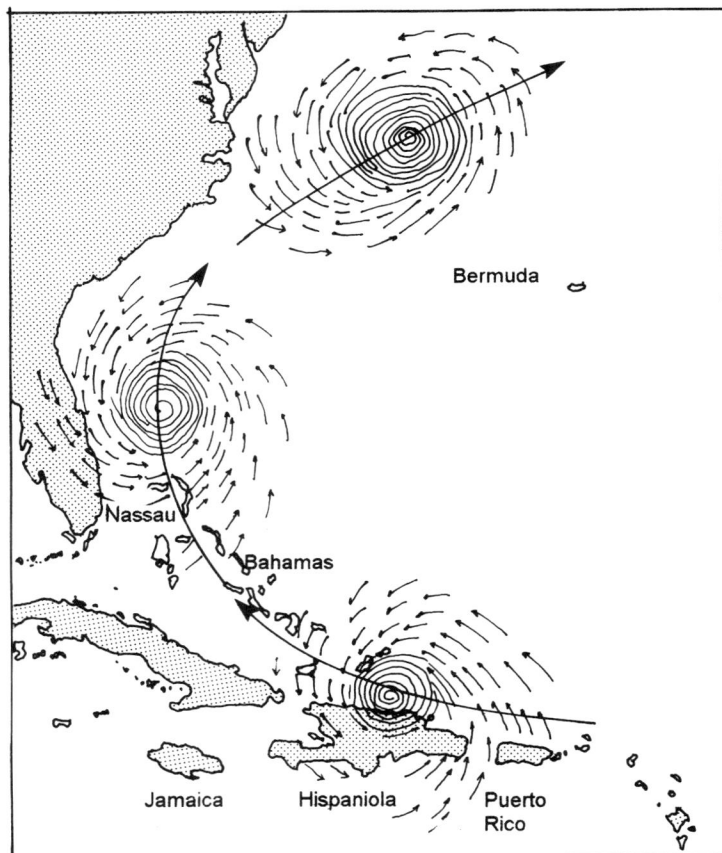

gusting of hurricane winds are certainly not static loads. Hurricanes produce a noise level approaching that of a jet aircraft, and they send solid objects, both large and small, flying through the air. Hurricanes are sometime associated with winds ranging from 73 to 180 miles per hour, and in many cases these winds find the energy flow of construction in buildings, with devastating results. Given these conditions, the stability of the structure as a whole and the strength of its components must be taken into account.

West Indian hurricanes pass in the vicinity of Jamaica approximately once in two years. The majority of them cause little more than heavy rain and fresh to strong winds. An occasional hurricane from the Atlantic on a westward course is destructive there. The island lies a little to the east of the most frequent paths of western Caribbean storms.

Earthquakes

The island of Jamaica consists essentially of an east-west core of serpentine white limestone, which is surrounded by shale and many different igneous, sedimentary, and metamorphic rocks, which were folded and uplifted at the end of Cretaceous time.

The center and west of the island has been uplifted in stages to form several distinct plateau surfaces. Since then, the water-soluble limestone has been eroded by many rivers, leaving a landscape of sharp, crested ridges and deep, twisting valleys. Where the limestone still remains, as it does over at least half the island, the landscape varies from place to place.

Seismic disturbances have occurred frequently in Jamaica since its settlement, but in general, the shocks have been slight. In 1692, however, a severe earthquake took place, engulfing parts of the city of Port Royal built on the sand spits across the harbor opposite the present site of Kingston and seriously damaging smaller areas built on the limestone reef. Kingston is located on the south side of Jamaica on the seaward edge of a large alluvial fan, occupying a V-shaped reentrant in the mountains.

In the 200 years following this great earthquake, the island was shaken from time to time by minor disturbances, some of which were moderately intense, but no record seems to have been kept until the latter part of the 19th century. Between February 19, 1880, and November 25, 1906 (when records were available), 163 shocks were recorded. These disturbances were greatest in the autumn and winter months and least severe in the spring and summer months. There were 168 disturbances during the night (6 P.M. to 6 A.M.) compared to 150 during the day (6 A.M to 6 P.M). In the evening there was a

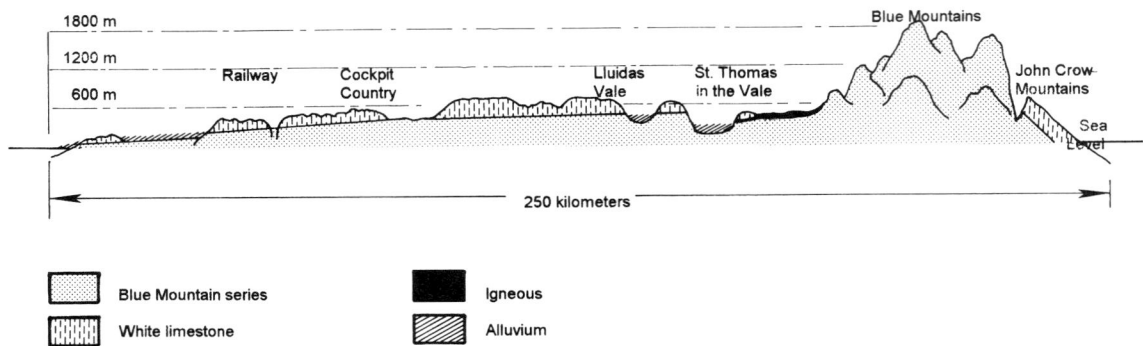

Sketch of a section across Jamaica to show the geology.

strong rise between 8 and 10 o'clock, followed by a falling off until 2 to 4 o'clock the following morning.

The rocky areas near Kingston are confined principally to the mountains, the narrow border of coastal plains consisting of unconsolidated materials. In the rocky areas, the surface is composed of disintegrated rock and stone, forming a mantle of talus over the hillsides. The slopes are often very steep, and as a result of the earthquakes, many boulders and avalanches were precipitated down the mountainsides. In many cases, trails were obliterated and roads ruined by slipping or by being covered by debris, and a few people were killed.

The Jamaican earthquake of January 14, 1907, was intense, and the destruction was correspondingly severe. While some tall buildings escaped complete demolition, nearly all were badly wrecked; in many cases, even one-story houses and stores were destroyed. The destruction was not uniform, however; it varied greatly according to the nature of the materials used in construction. In decreasing order of resistance, the structures were of steel, wood, stone, concrete, and brick.

CHAPTER 2

Hawaii

INTRODUCTION

The Hawaiian Islands are located in the middle of the North Pacific, just south of the Tropic of Cancer, on the same latitude as Mexico City, Calcutta, and Hong Kong. Today, more than 130 islands, islets, and shoals make up the Hawaiian Islands, stretching 1,600 miles across the North Pacific. Hawaii is the southernmost state of the United States and the most westerly, except for a few islands in the Alaskan Aleutians. Together the islands constitute 6,450 square miles of land. The eight major islands of Hawaii account for over 99 percent of the total land area and are home to 100 percent of the population (except for a staffed military installation here and there). From northwest to southeast, the islands consist of Niihau (privately owned), Kauai, Oahu, Molokai, Maui, Lanai, Kahoolawe (uninhabited), and Hawaii, the Big Island. The state has just over 1,000 miles of tidal shorelines and ranges in elevation from Mauna Loa's 13,796-foot summit to Maro Reef, which is often washed by the sea.

The Hawaiian Islands.

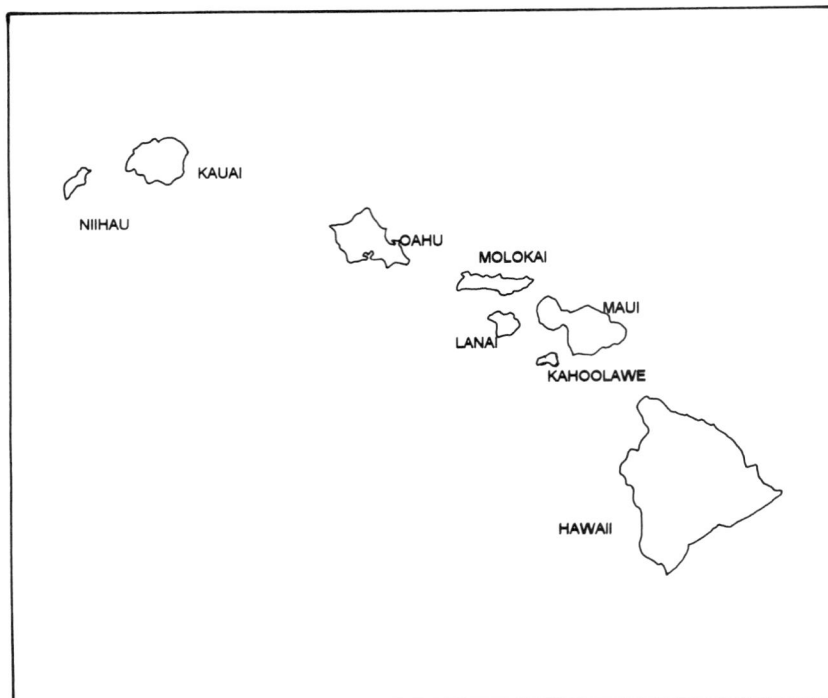

The Hawaiian Islands are the summits of a range of volcanic mountains that rises 18,000 feet above the floor of the ocean. These huge mounds of cooled basaltic lava are skirted by coral reefs, the skeletons of billions of polyps. Mauna Kea and Mauna Loa rise 14,000 feet above sea level, with a continuous slope that, if the water was removed, would make them the highest mountains in the world: nearly 32,000 feet high. The islands are separated from other land masses by broad stretches of deep ocean. It is over 2,000 miles to North America and over 4,000 miles to Japan and the Philippines.

Oahu, which means "gathering place," is partly tropical garden and part high-tech American city in the Pacific Basin. As a first-time visitor, I couldn't help being amazed at the island's diversity. Apart from the miles of endless beaches, the island has countless museums, a state library, botanical gardens, cultural classes, a major university, and an abundance of campsites. Geologically, Oahu is the second oldest main island after Kauai. It emerged from beneath the waves as hissing lava a few millions years after Kauai and cooled to form Hawaii's third largest Island.

Waikiki, one of the world's most famous beaches, is located on the island of Oahu, bordered by the Ala Wai Canal and running eastward to Diamond Head. Until 1901, when the Moana Hotel was built, this area was little more than a string of dirty beaches backed by a mosquito-infested swamp. Prior to that time, only Hawaii's few

Oahu.

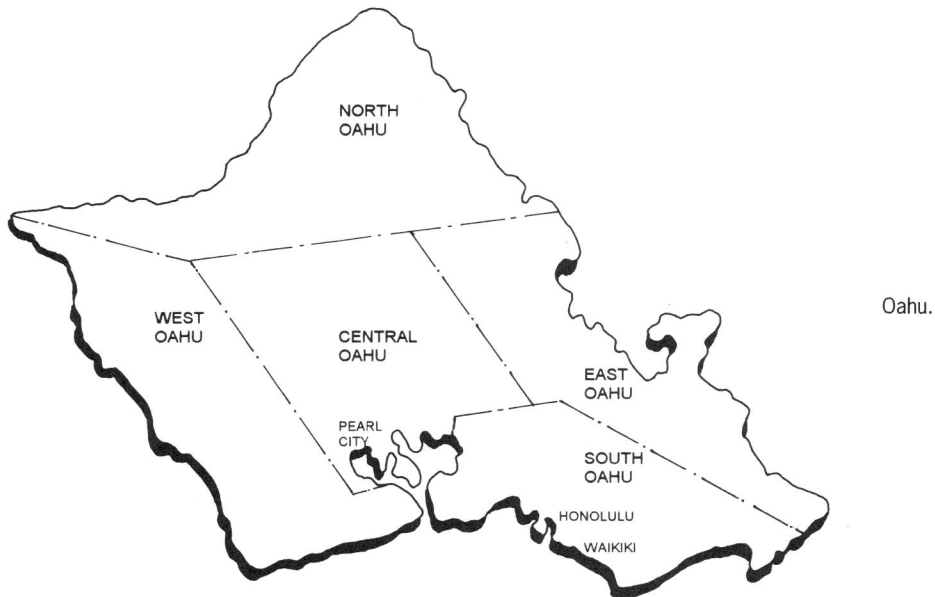

remaining ali'i* and a handful of wealthy Kama'aina† families had homes there. Today over 125 hotels and condominiums provide more than 35,000 rooms.

Downtown Honolulu is a mixture of quaintly historic and modern architecture. The center of downtown is Iolani Palace, the only royal palace in America. Within close proximity are the state capitol and other government buildings. Chrome and glass skyscrapers occupied by Hawaii's economically mighty overlook small stone and wooden structures of the 19th century.

Like the other Hawaiian islands, Oahu's weather is best described as just winter and summer, and even the peaks of these seasons have only moderate changes in temperature. The summer season runs from May to October, while the somewhat cooler, wetter season extends from November to April.

ARCHITECTURE AND CULTURE

Native Polynesian Hawaiians

The Polynesians first came to Hawaii 1,500 years ago, long before European sailors mustered the courage to leave their seacoast to venture out of sight of land. The Polynesians freely roamed the Pacific,

---

*The ali'i's are tribal kings and queens, and chiefs who derived power from the gods.

†Kama'aina is usually used to describe a native-born Hawaiian descended from the native chiefs or the missionaries.

without compass or sextant, in light canoes—twin canoes connected by a deck that carried fifty passengers or more, with a cargo of food and freight. They were guided by the stars, the prevailing winds, familiar cloud formations, and a sixth sense. They often sailed thousands of miles from home, such as the Marquess Islands and Tahiti. These were the navigators who discovered and colonized the Hawaiian Islands before A.D. 500—perhaps as early as A.D. 200.

The islands previously populated by the Polynesians in the South Seas were similar landfills. The Polynesians were masters at establishing a foothold on such stark shores, and their skills in husbandry were as good as their seamanship. They brought to Hawaii essential subsistence foods like taro, sugarcane, the South American sweet potato, breadfruit, a variety of coconuts, bamboo, gourds, dogs, pigs, fowl—and rats as stowaways. The Polynesians sailed between Hawaii and their homeland for hundreds of years, and great annual migrations took place over thousands of ocean miles. These voyages gradually diminished and then ceased altogether, possibly in an effort to avoid overpopulation. For at least 500 years the immigrants were on their own, independent of their South Seas relatives, completely isolated in the middle of the Pacific. Generation after generation passed and even some of the gods were forgotten, with ancestors remembered only in ancient chants recited by professional bands. The Polynesian dialect evolved through a form of unwritten language. The islanders multiplied prodigiously in their isolation. Old habits and practices changed. Communities grew into kingdoms and remained completely ignorant of the rest of the world.

Some forty or fifty generations had gone into the molding of Hawaii and Hawaiians. The work, the play, the climate, and the diet manifestly agreed with the descendants of the first Polynesian invaders, for by the 1700s little kingdoms existed on all the major islands, and the total population had swelled to a third of a million. Villages dotted the shores everywhere and crowded inland onto the plateaus. Cultivated lands extended deep into the valleys and up the bordering mountainsides, where slopes were terraced, the terraces packed with soil carried up from below, irrigated, and planted with taro, plantains, and sweet potatoes.

When the Hawaiians first came to these islands, they had to build their homes from the materials they found there. They had no lumber, as we have today, but they did have stone, timber, woven lauhala,* and pili grass. They made the best possible use of local materials, and these had an effect on the style of their houses. The

---

*Lauhala (the leaf of the pandanus) is used to make much of the plaited work, such as basket, mats, pillows, mat sails, sandals, and balls.

tools the Hawaiian used also had to be made out of what they found. There was no metal in Hawaii; every bit of metal found there today is imported. The original settlers, who were sailors, built their houses accordingly. Sailors do not use nails or pegs; instead, they tie and lash things together because, at sea, lashings hold better than nails or pegs. When they first landed, therefore, the colonists set up houses and lashed them together as a sailor would in a canoe.

In the beginning, there were no distinct classes of house builders, as the Polynesians were expert canoe builders or master

**Hawaiian Thatched Hut
Polynesian Cultural
Center
Laie, Oahu**

For hundreds of years before Captain Cook's arrival, ancient Hawaiians lived in simple grass huts. They provided shelter for a people who lived mostly outdoors and had few possessions. This *pili hale* (grass house) is a recreation of an ancient Hawaiian thatched hut.

**Hawaiian Thatched Hut
(Re-creation)
Polynesian Cultural
Center
Laie, Oahu**

Interior view—meeting hall.

**Hawaiian Thatched Hut (Re-creation)
Polynesian Cultural Center
Laie, Oahu**

Detail.

canoe cutters. There were some, termed *kuene hale,* who were skilled at putting up houses and who might be called to help. Every man built his own home (hale), with the assistance of his relatives and friends. "In the South Seas, however, house building was a distinct profession, practiced by expert carpenters who were organized into guilds or trade associations comparable to the trade guilds in China or medieval Europe" (Wise et al., 1965, p. 70).

After the housing site had been chosen, timber had to be cut and trimmed in the forest. The pili grass or lauhala had to be collected for thatching. Hau bark or morning-glory runners were gathered, rolled into great balls (like balls of twine) ready for use, and brought together with the other materials at the site. After the ground was cleared, the terrain would be leveled up by building low walls of stone and filling in with earth; sometimes the whole platform was built of stone. Then digging sticks were used to dig post holes at the corners and along the sides and ends of the leveled floor. The side posts were set up and the holes filled in with stones and earth that was firmly trampled down. The exterior framing completed, ready for thatching, looked like a very large birdcage. The rods to hold the thatching were spaced four fingers apart. Thatching was a long, tedious job that involved tightly binding every leaf of grass with bark or vine. At the ridge and roof corners, the grass had to be plaited tightly to prevent leaking. In cold regions such as Waimea, Hawaii, a fireplace was built in the middle of the floor. A shallow depression was made in the floor, walled with flat stones set on edge. There was no chimney, and the fireplace was never used for cooking.

Polynesian Hawaiians had different types of buildings for different occasions that were appropriate to the islands' climate and to their lifestyles. The *heiau* (temples) were open to the heavens and the elements, and were the most enduring and most culturally significant structures of the period. The *heiau* were raised platforms made of lava stone or coral rock filled with drums, gourds, and carved idols. These stone platforms were used by the *kahuna* (priests), who performed ancient religious ceremonies, including bloody sacrifices.

Some early Hawaiians lived in *hale pokahu,* or rock caves. Since the early Hawaiians lived mainly outdoors, their huts or caves were mainly used for storage and were used for shelter only when severe weather drove them inside.

Hale were mainly simple thatched huts built on raised stone foundations using coconut bark, pili grass, and woven lauhala. The floor of a good house on a stone foundation was covered with pebbles, but in poorer houses with earth floors, the ground was simply covered with dried potato vines, grass, and old mats. A fine house had beautiful heavy lauhala mats for floor coverings.

At its best, Polynesian architecture is appropriate in both design and function, makes good use of locally available materials, and is sensitive to the environment and climate. The climate of the Hawaiian Islands allows for a scattered housing arrangement rather than the modern style of packing dwellings close together on streets. The old way of living is evident today in Kona, where the houses are scattered all along the shore and along the road. This arrangement is also found in the vicinity of Honolulu, back in the valleys of Kalihi and Nuuanu, where the houses are scattered along in the valley bottom and on the hillsides—the healthy and natural way to locate homes in Hawaii. In early Hawaii, concentration of population for governmental and business purposes was not necessary. Small villages were established near good fishing grounds or in the vicinity of their taro and sweet potato plantations. The houses of the chief were generally built near the best fishing places, with his relatives and retainers as well as his workmen nearby. This allowed villages to grow up, mostly along the coasts.

When the British Captain James Cook came to the Hawaiian Islands in 1778, he found the village at Waimea, Kauai, and described it as a community of villages with "no appearance of defence, or fortification." Houses were "scattered about without any order" or pattern in relation to other houses. Cook further observed that there was no particular housing size, some dwellings being as large as 40 to 50 feet long and 20 feet wide, while others were minimal. They were "oblong corn or hay stacks" in shape, and most had no or very low side walls, resembling "a barn roof made of hay placed on the ground." The huts were well thatched with long grass and slender poles. Entrances were located at either ends or sides and were low, requiring one almost to crawl rather than walk in. Light entered through this opening, which provided a good retreat in bad weather. Floors were covered with dried grass, over which was spread mats to sit and sleep on.

When Captain Cook arrived, Kamehameha was forty-two years old and a veteran of many wars. (Kamehameha the Great was born on the island of Hawaii around 1736. He was the nephew of a rising noble, Kalaniopuu, and his mother was a chieftess of high rank. In 1782, he began what were known as the "Bitter Wars." Kamehameha made several successful armed sorties against the three main chiefs who opposed him, on his way to becoming conqueror of virtually his entire world and king of the Hawaiian Islands.) Cook named the islands the Sandwich Islands—for his naval patron, the Earl of Sandwich—and claimed them for the British Empire. Cook's discovery of Hawaii started a wave of new invasions, which changed the social order of the Polynesians and threw them into confusion and turmoil. Cook and his men introduced melons, pumpkin seeds, goats, and diseases to these isolated islands. The continued invasion added relentlessly to the disruption. Compared to other nations, which took 20,000 years to discard the last vestiges of the Stone Age and adapt themselves to standards of high living, in Hawaii this transition was compressed into a mere century and a half. Little by little the old Hawaiian culture was abandoned, submerged, or commercialized. Each group of invaders tried, with great success, to change the natives into their own (foreign) image.

The invaders tackled the terrain with great success and tried to improve on nature and the efforts of the native Hawaiians. They destroyed ancient landmarks and created new ones, turned deserts into verdant expanses, and converted grass hut settlements into cities, coral-strewn shore fronts into palmy beaches, mountains into fortresses, wastelands into playgrounds, treacherous bays into harbors, and inaccessible island outposts into popular tourist havens.

By 1794 the port of Honolulu was discovered by Western mariners and whalers. In 1803 or 1804, King Kamehameha I moved to Honolulu. His "palace" consisted of a compound of thatched huts close to the Heiau o Pakaka, approximately where Pier 12 stands today. Kamehameha the Great died at the age of eighty-two on May 8, 1819, in Kailua-Kona on the Island of Hawaii.

Missionaries and Their Congregationist Architecture

The arrival of Captain Cook in 1778 began a chain of events that would radically transform the way of life of the Hawaiians. News of the discovery traveled to Europe and America, and before long, other Westerners arrived, bringing their tools, artifacts, animals, and plants, their ideas and customs, and their diseases. Pacific trading flourished for Westerners from 1785 to 1870, first furs and then sandalwood, followed by whaling. The American traders carried furs from North America to China and silks, teas, and porcelains from China to Boston, New York, and Philadelphia. Hawaii was a convenient port for rest, recreation, and restocking. Soon traders learned that the forests of Hawaii were filled with sandalwood, prized by the Chinese for delicately carved boxes and sacred objects, as well as for incense and oil.

In 1819, having exhausted the whaling grounds in the South Pacific, whalers moved north to the sea off Japan. Japan had, however, closed its ports to foreigners, so they sailed south to Hawaii for reprovisioning and recreation. By 1850, Honolulu's sleepy villages had turned into bustling port towns.

The traditional Hawaiian religious system broke down as the Westerners, with their alcohol and prostitution, corrupted the Hawaiian way of life. By the time Protestant missionaries from New England arrived in 1820 to "save" the "natives," the *kapu* (taboo) system had already been officially abolished, leaving a religious void that the missionaries were only too eager to fill. The Congregationalist missionaries who had sailed for 168 days from Boston, along with physicians, teachers, printers, and their families, arrived on March 31 off the northern shore of Hawaii, at Kawaihae, after spending almost six months at sea.

On January 10, 1821, nine months after the missionaries brought Christianity to the Sandwich Islands, they introduced the first frame house ever to appear in Hawaii in the form of the colonial-style architecture seen throughout New England in the 18th and 19th cen-

Mission Houses 1821–1831 South King and Kawaiahao Streets Honolulu, Oahu

The materials used on the oldest surviving New England-style house in the islands were shipped from Boston in 1821. Structural members were measured and precut. Its small windows and short roof overhang were better suited to the climate of Massachusetts than to that of Hawaii. Later additions of the porch and balcony were regional improvements made in 1841 using local coral and salvaged ship lumber.

turies. Prepared in New England for rapid assembling, the building stood two stories high and would have looked appropriate on a village green. It housed the entire Honolulu mission, a room to a family.

The architecture of the imported frame house was inappropriate both in its design and in its materials. The small windows and clipped eaves of the house were designed for long New England winters and did not suit the year-round subtropical weather of Hawaii. The materials used for framing, shingles, and clapboard were oak, cedar, pine, and chestnut. These were all native to the New England area but had to be shipped from Boston to the Hawaiian Islands.

The second type of house, built in 1831, made adjustments for the local climate and indigenous materials. It utilized coral rocks from nearby reefs, with locally produced mortar and lumber from salvaged ships. Even though some of the lumber still had to be imported from Maine, this was the earliest use of indigenous materials for construction of an imported-style building. This two-story house had more and larger windows, with shutters to help keep out the heat. In 1835, the missionary Amos Starr Cook designed and built a one-room adobe schoolhouse to educate children of the ali'i. This is the only adobe structure of the period still standing today.

A coral block "bedroom addition" was made to the oldest frame house in 1841 to house the mission's print house. Later additions that year included a porch and a second-story balcony, which were adaptations to a more appropriate indoor-outdoor lifestyle. Lumber for the addition came from the ship *Ruby*, which lay aground on a reef near Honolulu.

The first 'Iolani Palace was built of wood in 1845. Until then, the royal family continued to live in grass-thatched houses, but they also acquired a number of Western-style retreats and residences during the first half of the 19th century. One of the finest homes of the missionary period, and the oldest continually occupied residence in Honolulu, is stately Washington Place.

Washington Place was built in 1846 for John Dominis, a ship captain, who moved to Honolulu from New York with his wife and young son, John Owen Dominis, who later married High Priestess Lydia Lili'uokalani, the sister of King David Kalakaua. Queen Lili'uokalani lived at Washington Place after being deposed by American annexationists in 1893. She returned to Washington Place following her nine-month imprisonment in 'Iolani Palace, where she lived until her death at age seventy in 1917.

By 1850, Honolulu had become the commercial capital of the Hawaiian kingdom and one of the least inviting places on earth. Its towns had become a sea of grass shacks accented here and there with imported foreign architecture. Except for the haystack houses, every structure, like the vegetation, seemed to have been borrowed from some other land.

For the most part, the sheds and warehouses at the landing duplicated the waterfront scene at San Francisco or San Diego. In the book, *The Island,* author W. Storrs Lee writes, "the church steeples, charity school belfry, and mission community were strictly New England. The new multiverandaed royal palace was a naive adaptation of British Victorian; Nantucket widow's-walks topped the dwellings of retired whaling captains; high-pillared Charleston porches fronted the stately retreats of successful merchants; and the dominant architectural accent in the business district was straight out of what was then Mexican (Southern) California, a western frontier setting of adobe shops, false-front stores complete with narrow stoops and hitching posts" (p. 149).

Nowhere was this evidence of the slow transformation of Honolulu from an unattractive native village into an even less attractive Pacific marketplace more striking than on the harbor front.

The Monarchy Period

The economic and political powers of Hawaii's royal rulers continued to weaken during the second half of the 19th century due to the impact of the American missionaries and wealthy businessmen. In fact, when King Alexander Liholiho and Queen Emma left Ka Hale Pule, the Kawaiaha'o Church, and embraced the Anglican Church in 1861, they clearly expressed their loss of faith in American Protestant missionaries, planters, and traders. They also looked to the monarchies of Europe for new political and economic alliances. The exposure to cosmopolitan goods and ideas infected the islands' monarchs with new appetites for European art, elaborate Victorian furniture, Chinese silks, and foreign foods and fashions. The attraction of faraway capitals was so great that some royals took to the sea after centuries of national isolation.

This influence is manifested in the neoclassical architecture of Honolulu's capital district, which remains the enduring legacy of the monarchy period. The Royal Mausoleum (1865) was built by Lot Kamehameha V following the deaths of his brother, Alexander Liholiho Kamehameha IV, and his nephew, Prince Albert. 'Iolani Barracks (1870), Kamehameha V Post Office (1871), Ali'iolani Hale (1874), Lunalilo Tomb (1876), and 'Iolani Palace (1882) were all built by the monarchs to house the royal family or to shelter the island kingdom's bureaucracy. The English Gothic St. Andrew's Cathedral was built under the direction of Queen Emma, who established the Church of England in Hawaii. The Italianate-style 'Iolani

Iolani Palace 1882
417 South King Street
Honolulu, Oahu

Iolani Palace shows the influence of the European architectural style on Hawaiian royalty in the mid-19th century. The most historically significant and architecturally interesting building of the monarchy period, this Renaissance Revivalist structure was the residence of King Kalakaua until his death in 1891. The Iolani Palace is the only royal palace in the United States. The building is constructed of brick and stucco over a skeletal steel structure.

Palace was built by King Kalakaua, the "Merry Monarch," in 1882 at a cost of $360,000. The monarchy period—the forty-two years between 1851 and 1893—was an era of dramatic political changes and tragedies for the Kamehameha and Kalakaua dynasties. During these four decades, the throne passed five times and the monarchy of the Kingdom of Hawaii was weakened and finally overthrown.

The Territorial Period

The decade following the overthrow of the Hawaiian monarchy in 1893 was a period of economic boom in the sugar industry that led to a boom in construction in the islands, especially Honolulu. The growth of the sugar

Ali'iolani Hale 1874
South King and Mililani Street
Honolulu, Oahu

Ali'iolani Hale, thanks to the television series *Hawaii Five-O*," is one of the most widely recognized buildings in Honolulu. The ionic columns, arched entrance and windows, and exterior walls imitating European cut stone give the building its neoclassical look. The 18-foot bronze statue of Kamehameha 1 standing in front of the building is a duplicate of the original, which was lost at sea near Cape Horn on its way to Hawaii from Europe.

Iolani Barracks 1870
South King and Richards
Streets
Honolulu, Oahu

Iolani Barracks, also called
Hale Koa or Warriors House,
was built for the Royal
Household Guard and their
families. The castle-style
building is unique in the
islands, with 18-inch-thick
walls constructed from
4,000 coral blocks cut from
Honolulu reefs. The building
was moved, block by num-
bered block, to its current
site of the Iolani Palace
grounds.

industry was due mainly to treaties that permitted duty-free Hawaiian
sugar imports to the United States. This expansion was supported by
continuing waves of immigrant laborers for the plantation owners.

The military importance of Hawaii was quickly realized in 1898,
after U.S. annexation, in terms of infrastructure construction. By
1919, Pearl Harbor was fully operational as a naval base, complete
with dry-docking and repair facilities. The influx of military person-
nel following the 1898 Spanish-American War, as well as shiploads

Harkness Nurses Home
1932
1301 Punchbowl Street
Kewalo, Oahu

This was originally designed
as a residence hall for the
students nurses of Queens
Hospital.

Honolulu Academy of Arts   1927
900 South Beretania Street
Honolulu, Oahu

The Honolulu Academy of Arts provides a regional design response with many residential qualities. The building has a massive tile "Hawaiian" roof, a shaded entrance arcade, textured masonry exteriors, and an Oriental pavilion interior plan.

of immigrant workers arriving regularly to provide plantation labor, swelled the population of the new Territory of Hawaii to 141,000 by the turn of the century. Honolulu's population grew especially rapidly—from 14,000 in 1890 to 40,000 by 1900—creating a demand for new construction as business and commerce also increased rapidly.

The Territory of Hawaii experienced two decades of rapid population growth beginning around 1920, increasing from 256,000 to 423,000 in 1940. Most of the growth occurred on Oahu, where it was concentrated around Honolulu. Almost a full century after the New England missionaries landed in Hawaii, its architecture reached an unprecedented level of excellence in design and construction techniques.

Plantation Architecture

With the depletion of the Pacific whaling grounds by 1865, the replacement of whale oil by petroleum, and the demand for sugar in the United States, the cultivation of sugarcane—grown commercially since 1835—had become Hawaii's dominant industry. The Great Mahele (land division) of 1848 ended the native system of communal land tenure and allowed sugar planters to buy, lease, or otherwise control vast tracts of land.

The Masters and Servant Act of 1850 made it legal to import contract laborers (a practice that continued until the United States annexed Hawaii), which enabled planters to meet the labor demands of the newly developed plantations. A combination of Hawaiian migration to California during the gold rush, Hawaiians signing on as seamen on whalers, and Western diseases such as measles, whooping cough, mumps, influenza, leprosy, and smallpox drastically reduced the Hawaiian population from possibly almost a million to about 82,000 in 1850. Western diseases (to which native Hawaiian lacked immunity) killed hundreds of thousands of Hawaiians. In addition, those who remained were unwilling to provide long hours of backbreaking labor on the plantations. Plantation owners, who wanted cheap, obedient workers for their expanding industry, searched worldwide for them.

Plantation architecture grew out of an immense need to house the influx of foreign laborers who immigrated, mostly from China, Japan, Korea, Puerto Rico, and the Philippines to work the sugar and pineapple plantations on all the major islands. Plantation houses of this period were built according to a basic box plan, usually with a front porch or an open verandah along one side. Typically, they were roofed with a "Hawaiian" sloped tin roof, with double-hung windows, attic louvers (for ventilation), and raised floors.

Chinese Influence

The first group of laborers to be imported were Chinese, who began arriving in 1850 to work on sugar and rice plantations and mills. However, although the Masters and Servants Act permitted the importation of contract laborers in 1850, it was not until the 1870s that the Chinese began going to Hawaii in large numbers. In all, about 46,000 arrived before annexation. Of those who arrived before annexation, 95 percent were males; only after more Chinese women arrived in Hawaii, between 1890 and 1910, did a second generation of Chinese Hawaiians emerge.

Spanish/Portuguese Influence

Portuguese from the Azores and the Madeira Islands, arriving from 1878 to 1887 and from 1906 to 1913, were the second major ethnic group recruited for sugar plantation work. The more than 17,500 Portuguese who came consisted of families because the Portuguese government allowed recruitment on the condition that women and children be included.

Chinese Society Building (Re-creation)   1909
Hawaii's Plantation Village
Waipahu, Oahu

The result was a higher birth rate among the Portuguese compared to the Chinese, so that by 1910 Portuguese outnumbered Chinese in Hawaii. Between 1903 and 1905, 8,000 Spaniards, both families and single men, arrived, though many of them quickly left for California. Over 5,600 Puerto Ricans, both families and single men, arrived in 1901–2 and 1921.

Japanese Influence

The Japanese followed the Portuguese. Between 1885 and 1924, about 180,000 Japanese arrived in Hawaii, becoming by 1900 the largest ethnic group in the Hawaiian Islands. Accompanying the mass of laborers were small numbers of professionals and business-men: doctors, bankers, dentists, inspectors, and interpreters. Living and working conditions varied from plantation to plantation and gradually improved, especially after Hawaii became a territory of the United States. The plantation provided free housing, usually in camps segregated by ethnic group. As new groups joined the work-force, plantation managers constructed new camps for them. Each camp had a long building, and several people lived in each room of the building. The rooms were just huts, lined up row after row, con-taining clothes. There was no kitchen in the house since the laborers were almost all young single men. Single men stayed together in the big rooms, whose bunks rose in tiers against the walls. Sometimes single men had to live in the smaller rooms of married couples.

The arrival of Soryu Kagahi of the Hongwanji mission in 1889 marked the beginning of Buddhism in Hawaii. Kagahi traveled from

Japanese Duplex (Re-creation) 1910 Hawaii's Plantation Village Waipahu, Oahu

plantation to plantation on the island of Hawaii to comfort the Japanese; with money he collected from them, he laid the foundation for a temple in Hilo. Buddhism flourished despite the opposition of Christian ministers due mainly to the philosophy of Buddhist teachings. Like their Christian counterparts, Buddhist priests not only ministered to the spiritual needs of the Japanese, but performed other needed services as well. Like the Christian ministers, they wrote letters for laborers, acted as go-betweens in marriage, and helped settle family problems and disputes between management and labor. Christian leaders were angry at plantation managers for promoting Buddhism. Christian ministers struggled to convert the Issei, the first generation of Japanese in Hawaii, with little result, and the availability of Buddhist priests and temples made their task more difficult.

Japanese temple forms, based on Buddhist architecture introduced to Japan from China and Korea, were translated and adapted to the islands. The most recognizable Buddhist temple roofs are the hipped and gable irimoya styles. Other "Japanese" temples, such as the Honpa Hongwanji Temple or Jodo Mission in Honolulu, consist of hybrid Indian, Muslim, and Hindu architecture and utilize atypical materials such as concrete and stucco. Temples typically are elevated and made of natural wood. In fact, in some parts of Japan, Shinto temples are rebuilt every twenty years, replicating the style and types of wood. Shinto temple architecture frequently can be identified by *chigi,* **X**-shaped beams, and *katsuogi,* short tapered logs, seen on roof ridges. In addition to temples and shrines, Japanese designs and architecture are seen in residences and traditional-style restaurants.

Japanese Temple Building 1910 Honolulu, Oahu

The Statehood Period (American Influence)

U.S. statehood came to Hawaii in 1959, starting a new era of growth. Most of the Americans who went there were from California, and most of them went by boat. The relaxed Hawaiian way of life, with its addiction to sea, surf, and song, the everyday holiday spirit, the colorful, informal garb, and the blending of indoors and outdoors began spreading across the United States. Years of exposure to Oriental and Polynesian architecture, landscaping, and decoration had inspired island builders to translate many of these features into Western structural style and produce distinctive Hawaiian hybrids, which were being freely mirrored on the mainland.

Craftsman House
Makiki Heights, Oahu

Hawaii State Library
1913
478 South King Street
Honolulu, Oahu

**Hawaii State Capital
Building   1968
Beretania and Punchbowl
Streets
Honolulu, Oahu**

**Hale Kuahini   1962
East-West Road,
University of Hawaii
Manoa, Oahu
(I.M. Pei. Associates and
Young and Henderson)**

Hale Kuahine is a women's
residence hall providing living quarters for 120
women.

In the following years, tourism rose significantly with the first jet
airplanes landing in Honolulu, cutting flying time from the West
Coast to four and one-half hours. The 1960s and 1970s saw a ram-
pant development of resorts and condominiums in Waikiki, which
harmed the quality of the architecture in Hawaii. The regional
approach to designing residences and buildings to take advantage of
trade winds was lost with the introduction of air conditioning. It was
not until 1976 that the Honolulu City Council established the
Waikiki Special Design District. Antidevelopment activists, as well
as professionals and other citizens, continued to protest against
Waikiki's development in the 1990s.

**Board of Water Supply Building   1958
630 South Beretania Street
Honolulu, Oahu**

The Board of Water Supply's Public Service Building is constructed of reinforced concrete. It is connected to the 1939 Engineering Building by an overpass footbridge spanning Lisbon Street. The concrete façade of the building casts everchanging shadows throughout the day.

**Thomas Jefferson Hall 1962
East-West Road, University of Hawaii Manoa Campus, Honolulu, Oahu
(I.M. Pei, Associates and Young and Henderson)**

Designed in the international style, the building exemplifies balance and regularity of form, as well as the use of steel, concrete, and glass materials. It is complemented by an exceptional Japanese garden behind, designed by Landscape architect Kenzo Ogata.

Today, the first thing travelers see is usually the long row of highrise buildings on Waikiki Beach. The city has now become a place of skyscrapers and souvenir shops, tour buses, and the biggest hotels in the world. It's a bustling city with an ethnic mix that makes it different from almost any other city in the world.

Contemporary Architecture

Today's architecture reflects a renewed interest in the regional style of the territorial period. An expression of the Hawaiian style popularized in the 1920s by C. W. Dickey, reflecting the unique cultural and environmental characteristics of Hawaii, is once again being demanded by the community, and most architects are more than willing to oblige. This expression of a renewed interest in appropriate indoor-outdoor designs is evident in the Mediterranean-style masonry structure that is once again in favor. Today's high-quality residential, commercial, and resort structures again feature high ceilings and large openings to reveal ocean and mountain vistas and to welcome trade winds inside.

CLIMATIC DATA

The climate of the Hawaiian Islands is very consistent, with only moderate changes in temperature throughout the year. This regularity is due to the year-round warm sea surface temperatures, which keep the overlaying atmosphere warm as well. Actually, there are only two seasons here: the summer months (called *Kau* in Hawaiian) that extend from May to October and the winter months (*Ho'oilo*) that run from November to April. The average daytime summer temperature at sea level is 78°F. Nighttime temperatures are approximately 10°F lower. The shielding effect of the volcanic mountains and the differences in weather found at various elevations create many different climate zones. These consist of a diverse collection of microenvironments, each possessing unique weather, plants, and animals. It is not unusual to see tropical rain forests, cool alpine regions, stony deserts, and sunny white sand beaches, all within the span of a few miles.

The cooling effect of trade winds, low humidity, high pressure, clear sunny days, negative ionization from the sea, and an almost complete lack of industrial polution combine to make Hawaii not only the most healthful spot in America but one of the most comfortable places on earth. The weather remains just about the same throughout the year and depends more on where you are on any given island than on what season it is.

Waikiki Landmark Building   1993
Kalakaua Avenue and Ala Wai Boulevard
Waikiki Beach, Oahu

The thirty-eight-story Waikiki Landmark Building, a mixed-use property, incorporates a five-story, 60-foot truss bridge (the highest bridge in the state) connecting the two 320-foot towers and containing eighteen penthouse units. The structure is built on a foundation of concrete piles and reinforced concrete slabs with a curtain wall façade of imported French glass and Italian Rosa Porrino granite.

**Outrigger Canoe Club
1963
2909 Kalakaua Avenue
Waikiki Beach, Oahu**

Located below Diamond Head on Sans Souci beach, this unique reinforced concrete structure consists of a series of indoor and outdoor landscaped spaces with varying levels and ceiling heights flowing into one another, eventually opening to the beach and the Pacific Ocean.

**House
Diamond Head Road
Diamond Head, Oahu**

Temperature

The average daytime temperature throughout Hawaii is about 80°F, with the average summer day raising the thermometer only 7 degrees to 87°F. Nightime temperatures drop less than 10°F. Altitude, however, does reduce temperatures about 3.5 degrees for every 1,000 feet. The lowest temperature ever recorded in Hawaii was atop Haleakala in January 1961, when it dropped well below freezing to 11°F; the hottest day occurred in 1931 in the Puna District of the Big Island, with a scorching (for Hawaii) 100°F.

House
47-849 Kamehameha
Highway
Laie, Oahu

The daytime high temperatures in Honolulu during the summer range from an average of 85 to 87°F (29.4 to 30.6°C), with nighttime lows of 70 to 74°F (21.1 to 23.3°C). Winter daytime high temperatures in the city are 70 to 74°F (21.1 to 23.3°C), and nighttime lows are 65 to 69°F (18.3 to 20.6°C).

Average Temperature—Honolulu, Hawaii

	JAN	FEB	MAR	APR	MAY	JUN	JUL	AUG	SEP	OCT	NOV	DEC
(C)	22.7	22.7	23.3	24.1	25.0	26.1	26.6	27.7	29.4	26.0	24.9	23.3
(F)	73.0	73.0	74.0	75.5	77.0	79.0	80.0	82.0	85.0	79.0	77.0	74.0

Humidity

The trade winds also moderate the humidity. Hawaii has only a 50 to 60 percent daily humidity factor, much less than Hong Kong and Havana, which share the same location on the Tropic of Cancer.

Wind

The trade winds moderate Hawaii's temperature and keep it constant throughout the year. You can count on the trades to blow an average of 300 days per year: hardly missing a day during summer and half the time in winter. They blow throughout the day but are strong during the heat of the afternoon, when you need it most, and weaken at night. These breezes are so prevailing that the northeastern sides of the islands are always referred to as "windward," regardless of where the wind happens to blow on any given day.

House
47-200 Pulama Road
North East
Oahu, Hawaii

Throughout the year, The islands are affected primarily by high-pressure zones in the North Pacific that pump relatively cool, moist trade winds down onto the islands' northeastern slopes. This pattern is true for most of the summer and approximately half of the time in the winter. These winds are forced upslope by the mountain heights, where ultimately their moisture condenses into clouds that produce rain.

The trade winds moderate the temperature as the heat of the day rises and reaches a peak in the afternoon. As the evening turns to night and the temperature drops, the wind diminishes, only to start again the following day. Once or twice a year the trade winds stop completely and the wind switches around to come out of the south or west, bringing stormy or hot, sticky weather. Islanders call this *Kona weather.*

Kona in Hawaiian means "leeward," and when the trades stop blowing, these southerly winds often take over. *Kona winds* is a euphemism for bad weather, for it brings in hot, sticky air. The temperature drops slightly during the winter, so these hot winds are tolerable and even useful for moderating the temperature. In the summer they are extremely uncomfortable, but luckily again, they hardly blow during this season. A Kona storm is another matter. These subtropical low-pressure storms develop west of the Hawaiian Islands, and as they move east they draw winds up from the south, causing considerable damage to crops and real estate. There is no real pattern to Kona storms. In some years they come every few weeks, while in other years they don't appear at all.

Rainfall

Most of the rain falls in the mountains and valleys on the windward (northeastern) sides of the islands. The result is a rich tropical environment of flowers and verdant greens that have made Hawaii famous. The wettest months are from November to March, but these winter rains are usually very localized.

Average Rainfall—Honolulu, Hawaii

	JAN	FEB	MAR	APR	MAY	JUN	JUL	AUG	SEP	OCT	NOV	DEC
(mm)	86.4	66.0	71.1	33.0	25.4	4.1	15.2	15.2	17.8	50.8	66.0	88.9
(in.)	3.4	2.6	2.8	1.3	1.0	0.4	0.6	0.6	0.7	2.0	2.6	3.5

Landscape

The Hawaiians worshipped Pele, the fire goddess, whose name translates equally well as "volcano," "fire pit," or "eruption of lava." Pele spit fire and spewed lava that cooled and formed islands, which in turn attracted billions of polyps, whose skeletal remains cemented into coral reefs. The Hawaiian Islands, a perfect example of *shield volcanoes,* are formed by a succession of gentle submarine eruptions that build an elongated dome much like a turtle shell. As the dome nears the surface of the sea, the eruptions combine with air and become extremely explosive due to the rapid temperature change and increased oxygen. Once above the surface, they settle again and steadily build upon themselves. As the island-mountain mushrooms, its weight seals off the spewing fissure below. Instead of forcing itsway upward, the lava now finds less resistance by moving laterally.

Oahu has a total land area of 608 square miles and, measured from its farthest point, is 44 miles long by 30 miles wide. The two largest harbors in the state, at Honolulu and Pearl Harbor, are on Oahu. The island is divided along its entire length by the Koolau Mountain, creating windward and leeward sides. It is further divided on the northwest by the Waianae Range, which runs north-south, dividing the Waiana Coast from the massive Leilehua Plateau of the interior. Oahu's highest peak is Mount Kaola at 4,020 feet, which sits in the northern portion of the Koolaus. The hugh Leilehua Plateau is covered in pineapple and sugarcane, and lies between the two mountain ranges running all the way from Waialua on the north shore to Ewa, just east of Pearl Harbor.

Oahu's most impressive natural features were formed after the heavy volcanic activity ceased and erosion began to sculpt the island. The most obvious are the wall-like cliffs of the Poli Mountain heads, eroded by winds from the east, and the valleys cut by streams from the west. Diamond Head, Koko Head, and Punchbowl were created by three *tuff-cone* volcanoes after the heavy volcanic activities of early Oahu. A tuff cone is volcanic ash cemented together to form solid rock.

Hurricanes

The worst storms occur in the winter, and rains are heaviest in areas that are normally quite dry. Few destructive hurricanes have hit Hawaii in the last several decades. Hurricane Iniki, which battered the islands on September 11, 1992, had the greatest effect on Kauai and on the leeward coast of Oahu. With great ferocity, Iniki ripped ashore with wind speeds of up to 175 mph and slammed ashore on Kauai, virtually flattening or tearing to shreds everything in its path. Almost every structure on the island was damaged in some way. Yachts were heaped up on land like jangled toys, cars were covered over with red earth, at least one-third of all homes on Kauai (20,000) were broken into splinters, and 4,200 hotel rooms were destroyed. Fortunately, due to an effective warning system, only two lives were lost and fewer than 100 people were admitted to hospitals for injuries.

Earthquakes

Earthquakes are a concern in Hawaii and offer a double threat because they cause tsunamis. The Big Island, because of its active volcanoes, experiences hundreds of technical earthquakes every year, although 99 percent of them can only be felt on very delicate equipment. The last major earthquake occurred on the Big Island in late November 1975, reaching 7.2 on the Richter scale and causing millions of dollars worth of damage on the island's southern portion.

CHAPTER 3

Australia

INTRODUCTION

With an area of 2,968,000 square miles Australia is the smallest of the continents, but it is still enormous. It is comparable in size to the United States excluding Alaska. Australia's interior consists of 500 million acres of waste land that remains completely unused, a great expanse of desert and steppe country in the arid interior. In addition, there are 472 million acres of grazing land used for extensive stock farming. Besides the striking landscapes of the interior, Australia has many other attractions—endless beaches and, most spectacular of all, the Great Barrier Reef, the world's largest coral reef. The bulk of the population lives on the narrow, fertile eastern coastal plain and on the southeastern coast. The continent-long Great Dividing Range runs north-south down the eastern seaboard, separating the coastal plain from the drier inland areas.

Australian seasons are the opposite of those in Europe and North America, with summer starting in December, autumn in March, winter in June, and spring in September. Seasonal variations are not

Australia.

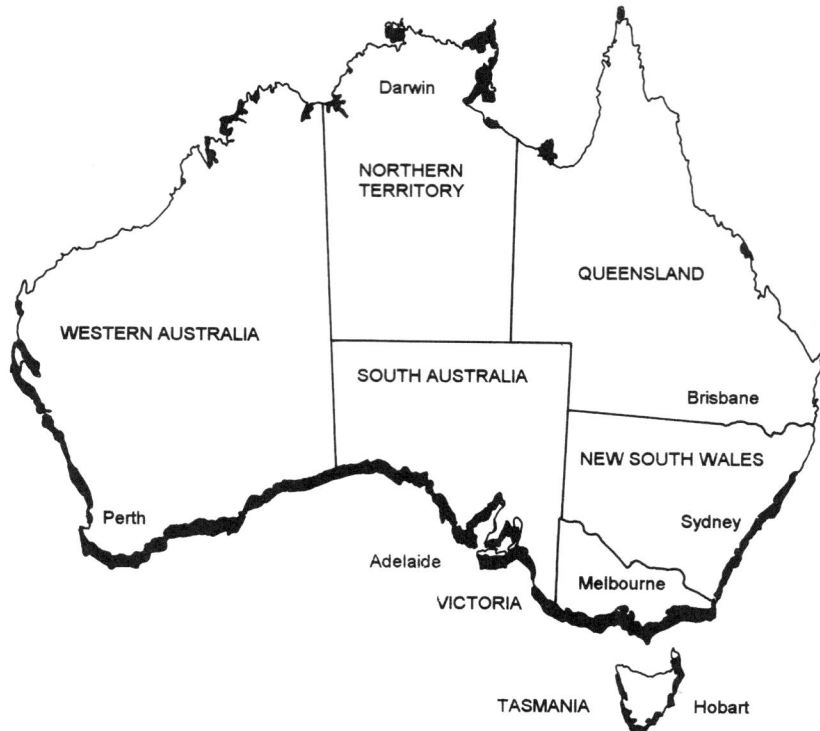

extreme, and it is rare for temperatures to drop below zero on the mainland except in the mountains. In the north, the seasonal variations become even less distinct. Darwin, in the far north, is in the monsoon belt, where there are just the two usual tropical divisions of hot, wet and hot, dry seasons. The wet season is mainly in the summer months, and the wettest months are January, February, and March. The southern states are more comfortable during the summer months, but the best times to enjoy the outdoors are the border seasons of spring or autumn, when the weather in the south is mild, Queensland is still warm, the humidity is not too high in the north, and there are fewer flies in the bush. On the coast the rainfall is often abundant, but temperatures are prevented from becoming low by the moist atmosphere and from becoming very high by the rain and cloudiness. Inland, however, conditions are drier, and the range of temperature from early morning to afternoon increases with the distance from the coast.

ARCHITECTURE AND CULTURE

The Aborigines

Australian aboriginal society has the longest continuous cultural history on earth, with its origins dating back to the last ice age. The original inhabitants of the continent are one of the best-known and least-understood people in the world. In reality, aboriginal culture, as anthropological work over the last 100 years has revealed, is a complex, subtle, and rich way of life. Aborigines have occupied Australia for at least 40,000 years. They came originally from Southeast Asia, entering the continent from the north.

Because of their relative cultural isolation, aborigines were forced to develop their own solutions to the problems of human adaptation in the unique and harsh Australian environment. The result was a stable and efficient way of life. Probably because of its effectiveness, the society was slow to change, especially technologically. The archaeological record reveals, however, a number of innovations, among them the earliest known human cremations, some of the earliest rock art, and certainly the first boomerangs, ground axes, and grindstones in the world.

The population of Australia at the time of the arrival of the whites in 1788 was probably between 250,000 and 500,000. The pattern of aboriginal settlement was like that of present-day Australians, except in the tropical north, with most of the population living along the coasts and rivers. Residential groups ranged in size from 10 to 50 people, with some temporary ceremonial gatherings reaching up to 500. Smaller local groups were the basic units of aboriginal society. These groups shared cultural traits and had economic and ceremonial dealings with other groups, but they did not form large confederations for such purposes as warfare or conquest.

The explorers Cook and Banks saw the aborigines as they had always been, in a state of balance with nature, able to survive without extreme neurosis or fear, without clothes and, in some regions, without houses. Apart from their northern origin, no one knows exactly who these Pleistocene colonists were. Whoever they were, they spread south, east, and west across the continent, killing giant kangaroos as they went. Their first campsites were drowned by the waters of the Timor Sea and the Gulf of Carpenteria, which rose so fast between 13,000 and 16,000 B.C. that they moved the coast inland at a rate of 3 miles a year. The Australian aborigines were almost destroyed by cholera and influenza germs brought by the European convicts. By 1789 their corpses were a common sight, huddled in the salt grasses and decomposing in the creamy hollows of the sandstone.

To the Iora aborigines of northern Australia, fire was shelter. That was part of the necessary logic of their lives, since to survive at all, the small family groups that made up the tribe had to migrate easily and rapidly over a wide area, feeding as they went, and that made the idea of solid, permanent dwellings inconceivable. To them, the hearth was far more significant than the home. A fire stick made the hearth portable. They used what they could find as dwellings: the sandstone caves of harbor shores, with sheets of bark propped up to form crude humpies. Caves and bark humpies got cold at night. The Iora therefore slept huddled together close to their ever-smoldering campfires, and accidental burns were common. In colder weather they lived in caves, in shelters of overhanging rock, and in hollowed-out trees, but sometimes they constructed buildings of grass, thatch, and bark stripped from eucalyptus trees.

Beehive-shaped structures made of saplings and mud may still be seen in the northeastern part of south Australia, and similar huts made of grass and saplings are used on the northern Kimberly coast. These huts have a very small opening that serves as a door and can be closed up, or a smoke fire may be lit near it to keep the mosquitoes out. The usual type of native hut is simply a matting of saplings and branches or a mere lean-to. Huts were sometimes constructed using raised poles interlaced with a variety of materials to form a thick wattling for the wall surfaces. One practical reason for raising the building would be to improve ventilation or avoid local flooding from tropical downpours, or possibly these structures acted as deterrents to the snakes, crocodiles, and other reptiles that frequent these regions.

Some aborigines today do build huts more substantial than the native types; they are an adaptation of the government houses (which seldom suit their needs), built in their traditional form. Among the best are some made of light timber and paper-bark, square in shape, fastened where necessary with wire. It appears, then, that the ideal Australian building type would be one intermediate between the indigenous type and simple Caucasian structures.

The British

Europeans began arriving in Australia in the 16th century: Portuguese navigators were followed by Dutch explorers and the English pirate William Dampier. Captain James Cook sailed the entire length of the eastern coast in 1770, stopping at Botany Bay on the way. After rounding Cape York, he claimed the continent for the British and named it New South Wales.

In 1779, Joseph Banks (a naturalist on Cook's voyage) suggested that Britain could solve the problem of overcrowding in its prisons by transporting convicts to New South Wales. In 1787, the first fleet set sail for Botany Bay under the command of Captain Arthur Phillip, who was to become the colony's first governor. The fleet comprised 11 ships, 750 male and female convicts, 4 companies of marines, and supplies for two years. For the new arrivals New South Wales was a harsh and horrible place, and the threat of starvation hung over the colony for at least sixteen years.

Buildings in Australia were erected with a sense of urgency not seen in Jamaica or any other colonies. Not only did the convict settlers lack the skills, tools, artistry, and craftsmanship necessary to build in the new territory, but starvation was a constant threat for the new arrivals because of their unfamiliarity with what the aborigines thought to be abundant land. The only good building timber came from the cabbage-tree palms that grew in profusion around the stream at Sydney Cove. They were straight, easy to work, and had little natural taper. All were cut down within a year. Construction in the beginning took a rudimentary form often consisting of simple pole structures, using the knowledge and techniques learned from the aborigines. Roofs were generally hipped and covered with bark or split timber shingles. The huts the settlers built were about 9 by 12 feet, with two windows like eyes on either side of a doorway. Their construction was equally simple. Walls were framed with 6-inch-square timber posts set directly in the ground; vertical studs 3 feet apart went between them. Between the roughly rabbeted studs, the carpenters inserted horizontal lengths of sapling whose ends were tapered to fit groves. The walls at this stage looked like crude washboards. Then they were daubed (roughly sealed) on both sides with mud. This method of construction was used in every peasant community in England and Ireland and throughout the colonies in the Caribbean (called *wattle and daub*). The usual roof was reed thatch gathered from the tidal marshes of Rushcutter's Bay. Later, it would be replaced by shingles. But when the winter rains came, the mud washed out of the walls.

The kitchen block was detached and became one of the outbuildings because of the fear of fire. This arrangement spawned the vernaculars, which, due to their additive quality, were joined together by covered ways or verandahs. The verandah, coupled with the hipped roof, became typical of Australian architecture. Wide verandahs became the setting for most social occasions. During hot nights the verandah was the place where the household slept. It was a living room as well as a study and play area. Until the 1850s, verandah roofs were supported either by turned timber columns with simplified Tuscan capitals or by simple square timbers.

Timber was almost universally used in the tropical north to construct houses, which were built on platforms. These were 6 to 10 feet above the ground with encircling verandahs, much like those of the Javanese in Indonesia, where their indigenous architecture is also raised above the ground. Although the reason for this style is unclear, improving ventilation or avoiding local flooding from tropical downpours are possible explanations.

Public Buildings—Georgian Style

As the Australian colony grew in prosperity, more permanent building materials, such as brick and stone, were needed for important government and commercial buildings. Before long, suitable clay was found and a convict, James Bloodworth, who had been a brickmaker in England, took charge of manufacturing. Convicts ground clay with water in natural depressions in the sandstone, using a log for a pestle; then, in barelegged teams, they squelched and trod it into a homogeneous mixture of clay and water. The bricks were molded, racked, dried, and fired. They shrank unequally, and nobody could build level courses with them. For mortar, the only source of lime was burned oyster shells, laboriously gathered by convict women. These supplied just enough lime for a permanent Government House, a two-story brick building with a tile roof, stone quoins, and real glass windowpanes—the first true piece of Georgian architecture in Australia. These government houses were composed of common Attic orders with a pediment in front. Imported Welsh slate was reserved for the prestigious public buildings; split timber shingles still remain the most popular roofing material. All other buildings had to be constructed without mortar, and instead were made with a mixture of sheep hair and mud. No ruins of the earlier convicts' buildings have survived at Sydney Cove.

Commodities in the new world were always in short supply, and the most sought-after commodity of all was rum. In the little community (fewer than 5,000 people in 1799, about 7,000 in 1805, just over 20,000 by 1817), nearly all the men and most of the women were addicted to alcohol. In Australia, especially between 1790 and 1820, rum became an overriding social obsession. Many colonists drank with a haunted thirst, determined to blot out the harsh reality of their lives. Because most convicts would rather be paid in rum than anything else, it gave great leverage to the wealthy landowner, who could secure any amount of overtime labor with a barrel. Few convicts felt that their rights were violated if their masters paid them partly in rum, and none complained about it.

The man who cleaned up the system was Lachlan Macquarie (1762–1824), the last British proconsul sent to run New South Wales as a military autocracy. Macquarie's first act after becoming Governor General was to design, with his wife, a new hospital, a three-block building with wide verandas derived not from English Regency architecture, but from Macquarie's observations in India. It was by far the largest structure ever built in the colony. He financed it with rum, just as the New South Wales government, 150 years later, would finance its colossally expensive Opera House in part with lotteries. Two of its three blocks survive today: the first presentable Georgian public building in Australia.

Macquarie's next task was to find an architect to design the many public buildings for the new colony. He found one in a convict, Francis Howard Greenway (1777–1837), a descendant of generations of builders and stonemasons, trained as an architect, but a poor businessman. Practicing in Bristol, he went bankrupt, forged a contract, and received a death sentence, which, as usual by then, was commuted to fourteen years' transportation. When Macquarie found out about Greenway's arrival in 1814, he grew cautiously interested because of his own modest talents and tainted past experience in dealing with clients. Macquarie hesitantly put him in charge of designing and building all government works, beginning in 1816.

Over the next year, Greenway turned out for Macquarie a series of buildings that were uneven in quality, the best of which utterly transformed the architectural standards of the fledgling colony. The main ones were two convicts' barracks, the Female Factory in Parramatta (1819) and a masterpiece—the Hyde Park Barracks for men in Sydney (1819), together with several churches, notably St. Mathews in Windsor (1817–20) and St. James in Sydney (1820–24). The Female Factory kept at least some women off the Parramatta streets, although it was never large enough.

Such projects demanded skilled labor from bricklayers, masons, tilers, blacksmiths, glazers, and joiners. There was an equally great need for unskilled labor. From 1814 to 1820, the government took over some 4,600 of the 7,200 convicts arriving in Australia to provide its workforce.

Public Buildings—Classical Style

English church buildings were copied and replicated in conformity with the principles of the particular religious society in England. Most church buildings were designed based on existing English church plans in accordance with Gothic revival principles.

Many modest public buildings were constructed in the first major building program of the colony of New South Wales under Governor Macquarie. Greenway had a genius for turning the relative poverty of colonial architectural resources—the lack of skilled carvers, for instance—to good account. He concentrated on proportion and material texture rather than ornament: the simple use of Palladian bays, with plain pilasters—brick on the Barracks, tawny sandstone on church buildings—firmly stating the proportions of the walls. The materials and details were well suited to the hard clarity of Australian light, as well as the limitations of convicts' masonry skills.

Dwellings

Imported design has played a major part in the history of Australian architecture from the colony's settlement to the present. Building were often prefabricated in Britain and brought with the fleet to the various colonies. Such was the house for Governor Phillip, a simple prefabricated house that arrived in 1788.

Designs were selected from English pattern books, which were modified for local needs. The *cottage* was an especially attractive type, partly because of its picturesque connotations but also because it frequently included a verandah, which formed a buffer zone between the interior and the heat of the Australian summer sun.

In 1790 Simeon Lord, a juvenile convict, was transported to Australia for stealing several hundred yards of calico. By 1798 he had his own warehouse distributing rum, and by 1799 his first ship. In 1803 Simeon built himself a mansion in Sydney, the largest private house in the colony. It had three stories, a basement, and an elegant verandah carried on slender columns over the street; it was built of sandstone bound with imported mortar.

Australia's tropical houses were built in a variety of styles and sizes, ranging from small one- to two-room workers' cottages to enormous mansions. There was, however, a consistency of form evident throughout the region due to the limited range of building materials and building crafts employed in the construction of these houses. It has been suggested that the basic plan of a typical house, which consists of four or six rooms juxtaposed back to back or linked through a corridor, has its roots in the Georgian buildings in England. These would have been familiar to convict settlers, who transplanted the styles and later added a verandah as a concession to the local climate.

Free settlers began to be attracted to Australia over the next decades, but it was the discovery of gold in the 1850s that changed the face of the colony. The huge influx of migrants and several large gold fields boosted the economy and irrevocably changed the colonial social structures. Aborigines were ruthlessly pushed off their tribal lands as new settlers took up land for farming or mining. Early settlers in tropical regions adopted the Georgian plans and modified them appropriately, using timber rather than stone and brick as the main construction material.

The houses built in tropical Australia reflect a lifestyle that is a unique expression of the way people have adapted themselves to an environment vastly different from their historic European experience. The one- and two-story houses have a special vernacular charm with a distinctive character. They have vast, spacious rooms with very high ceilings and ventilators and access from all four sides. The important rooms are surrounded by a deep verandah, part of which is usually enclosed in order to accommodate cooking and washing facilities. The verandah and the secondary living rooms surrounding the main living areas provide valuable shade and protect the walls from the heat of the tropical sun.

Australia's tropical houses are essentially lightweight timber and iron structures that are primarily the product of special local circumstances and reflect the scarcity of local materials and building skills. There are very few stone and mud buildings in Australia's tropical regions, as these are labor intensive. Masonry is confined to important public buildings rather than used in domestic structures. The basic structure of these houses is a fairly standardized timber frame made up of 2×4 (50×100 mm) studs mortised into top and bottom plates. They are usually lined with specially shaped boards known locally as *chamfer boards*. These boards are nailed flush to the studs, and diagonal braces are left exposed on the outside. This practice is not exclusively Australian; it is widely used on English and American farms and other low-cost structures associated with outbuildings of major residential architecture.

Stud framing is essentially an extension of the earlier widely spaced uprights, whose intermediate spaces were filled in in a number of ways (including the use of straw boards, mud, timber, or brick walls). Saw milling operations made it possible to cut hardwood studs of lighter, more easily transportable sections and lengths that were more closely spaced. The reliance on metal was soon replaced by the use of precut timber, which was a more versatile building material and readily available in larger quantities, from more developed centers in the south and also from coastal townships of the north.

The Australian tropical house is often compared with the Indian bungalow, which was built by the English during their occupation of India during the colonial period of the 18th and 19th centuries. This model was a version of the Bengal double-roofed house, which, like its Australian counterpart, has four to six rooms back to back surrounded by a deep verandah.

During the 19th century, this bungalow was built in various shapes and can be seen in different parts of the world, including the Dutch colonies of Indonesia and in the Caribbean. The Spanish colonists in the southwestern United States developed a building style that is very similar to the Caribbean one and uses the adobe materials employed by the American Indians.

The builders of colonial domestic buildings throughout the 18th and 19th centuries, whether British, Dutch, French, or Portuguese, all used established models from their mother countries as building prototypes. The basic difference between their counterparts in tropical Australia was that the building materials used in these colonial houses were largely masonry and therefore had a considerable heat storage capacity. These materials took a long time to heat up during the day and therefore provided cool interiors.

Although many of these timber houses were built during the latter half of the 19th century and the early 20th century, they seem to have survived remarkably well. Many of them have been either demolished to make room for new buildings or altered to such a degree that they are hardly recognizable. The houses that have replaced them are very poor examples of brick veneer villas more suited to the cooler climates of the southern cities.

The 19th-century Australian shunned the sun, building his house to face south and surrounding it with wide verandahs. This habit survived in the countryside, which is hotter and often short of water. The modern suburban residence, however, faces north, and solar planning welcomes sunshine with large sheets of glass to provide warmth.

From Imitation to Independence

Australia became a nation when federation of the separate colonies took place on January 1, 1901 (although many of the legal and cultural ties with England remain). The end of World War II brought a flood of European immigrants, many of them non-British—from Greece, Italy, Yugoslavia, Lebanon, and Turkey. These groups have been supplemented by more recent influxes of immigrants from Asia. The immigrants have made enormous contributions to the country, enlivening its culture and broadening its vision.

**The Opera House
Sydney
Photographer:
Lee Askew III, FAIA**

After Australia became a nation, its sense of national identity from an architectural standpoint seemed to be reflected more in applied emblems, such as the use of kangaroos and emus rather than in any structural shift. Rapid growth in industrialization occurred in the early 1900s with the production of steel, although the first steel-framed building, which still depended on masonry walls for support, had appeared in Sydney and Melbourne ten years earlier. Offices, department stores, banks, and hospitals all utilized self-supporting steel frames. Skyscraper construction soon began to change the sky-lines of Australian cities following the 1929 Depression and the two world wars.

The decade after World War II saw a significant growth in build-ings other than domestic and industrial. The period from 1955 on saw an unprecedented upsurge in commercial building that trans-formed the appearance of all of Australia's cities. The greatest growth occurred in Melbourne. The growth of industry changed work pat-terns and spawned the development of industrial suburbs, which were tacked on to the sprawl of the larger capital cities.

By 1968, property development reached boom proportions as a result of several factors, including the discovery of new minerals, the growth of merchant banking, and the search for investment opportu-nities by Australian and foreign companies.

Modern Architecture

Few architects in Australia prior to World War II rejected ornament and adopted the fundamental principles of modernism. One excep-

Office Building
Sydney
Photographer:
Lee Askew III, FAIA

tion was Australia-born Harold Desbrowe-Annear, who was designing open-plan houses with plain white walls and low-pitched roofs from 1918 on. Modern architecture actually began in the domestic arena because the funds for large-scale commercial and public building programs did not exist. The houses represented postwar architects' early interpretation of modern architecture, which would eventually change the nature of the country's built environment.

Ordinary houses in Australia differ markedly from both British and North American houses and bear a strong resemblance to those of the Caribbean and other tropical regions. Australian private homes, much like Caribbean homes, almost always have only one story and are roofed with galvanized iron, less often with tiles. They often have one or more outside verandas or terraces attached. Though the actual floor space of an Australian home is probably, on the average, less than that of an American or Canadian one, the Australian house sprawls untidily and looks bigger because it covers much more ground.

During the 1960s, there was a call for an architecture more Australian than the pastiche of the international school. Consequent research into the history of Australian architecture resulted in a renewed interest in the Australian vernacular. This development was of great importance to contemporary architecture, and its influence is apparent in recent work.

Contemporary Architecture

Australia's unique architecture developed over the last 200 years from the old English vernacular tradition to a form modified by climate and social needs. The earlier buildings were influenced by the materials and building techniques of the Australian aborigines, particularly in their use of bark stripped from trees, grass tree thatch, or leaf roofs. In addition, many of the early architects and engineers were associated with India, and the Anglo-Indian bungalow architecture was adapted to Australian conditions.

The 1970s saw a gradual implosion of modernism and a more complex historical and cultural analysis of architecture. Australia's culture by this time included a broader range of Europeans, as well as a wider admixture of peoples from other parts of the world, including Asia. Each group brought it own style of architecture, which was heaped on the region upon demand. Consequently, there is no single Australian style of architecture; instead, there is a plethora of inventive responses to the interweaving demands of client, site, and climate. Admittedly, the influences are primarily from Western European countries and the United States.

In the book *Old Continent, New Building—Contemporary Australian Architecture,* edited by Leon Paroissien and Michael Griggs, the authors describe several approaches resulting in contemporary Australian architecture (pp. 33 and 34). In one approach, international forms and techniques are applied to varying Australian conditions, challenging the Australian cities and suburbs by confronting them with recognizable international examples. This approach acknowledges the Australian climate and uses local materials. Another approach reinforces the sense of place by using traditional materials and often traditional building methods. Although this approach works to establish an Australian identity, it still embodies general modern movement principles. It gets its inspiration from vernacular and anonymous architecture, which is a simple, natural, and unornamented response to the landscape. Examples include primarily 19th-century rural architecture, with its rough bricks, timber, galvanized iron, broad verandahs, and deep, sheltering roofs.

Australian architecture today reflects the paradox of a very young nation, with fewer than 15 million inhabitants, in a very old land that was virtually primeval until two centuries ago. From such a beginning, 200 years is not a long time for sympathetic architectural forms to evolve. The heat and damp of the tropical north produced a distinct architecture built upon poles with shaded lattice screens. The vast plains produced an architecture of steep-hipped roofs with encircling verandahs open for ventilation. The temperate to cold climates in Tasmania produced a brick and stone architecture of extreme simplicity, while some of the architecture, such as at Cooler Pedy, was built underground for climatic reasons.

The 19th century saw an adaptive process that produced a transformed version of European architecture that relates to both the history and place of Australia.

The 20th century saw the rejection of the traditional building type, and with its demise went much of the sense of Australian design.

By the mid-20th century the impact of the modern movement, with its geometric structures and notions of functionalism, gave rise to a new approach to architecture. In the name of "progress" the boom period saw the radical transformation or destruction of the inner cities, especially Sydney, which was replaced with a brick-and-tile, trade-based architecture creating an image that was specifically and identifiably regional. Some of the most interesting architecture of the 1970s consisted of new work in old structures. Obsolete warehouses, piers, mills, and factories were given new life with changed functions. The most ambitious ventures, however, occurred in the field of housing.

Australian architecture, although faithful to the climate and landscape, is highly influenced by oversees trends prevalent at the

Water Front Building
Sydney
Photographer:
Lee Askew III, FAIA

time. Streets, houses, service stations, airports, and stores are, on the whole, interchangeable with their British or American architectural equivalents. The Australian version does, however, give the impression of being more modern than that in Britain and less so than that in the United States.

CLIMATIC DATA

Australia, because of its global site and physical features, has a varied climate, generally without extremes. Over inland areas of Australia the range of temperature is 70 to 90°F (21° to 32°C). On the north coast and the Queensland coast the range is about 60° to 80°F (16° to 27°C).

Three broad climatic zones can be distinguished in Australia:

- A tropical zone to the north of the Tropic of Capricorn
- A subtropical zone to the south of the tropic
- A cool temperate zone in the extreme south (Victoria) and in Tasmania

Australia's climate is determined by its location in the subtropical high-pressure zone, which gives it clear, dry, and brilliant sunshine almost year round. At its greatest east-west extent Australia lies on the Tropic of Capricorn, exposed to hot, dry air masses, which makes it the hottest of all the continents. Within this great extent, average temperatures in the center and north of the country rise in January to over 86°F (30°C) and in much of the northwest to over 95°F (35°C). On the coast, these heat waves seldom last longer than three days due to the cooling effect of natural sea breezes.

The sea exerts a moderating influence on temperature, reducing the temperature difference between day and night and, to a lesser extent, between summer and winter. The direct influence of the sea is, of course, felt only in the coastal zones. Much more important is the cooling effect of onshore winds during the hot summer period. These winds (e.g., the "Fremantle doctor" in the Perth area) bring down the high afternoon temperatures.

Temperature

In temperature, Australia ranges from the cool temperate climate of its southeastern extremity, Tasmania, to the extremely hot climate of those parts of Western Australia that lie along the Tropic of Capricorn. In general, though winter nights can be cold indeed over large parts of Australia, this continent is to be classed as ranging from warm to hot. Even in Melbourne, where a fire can be a comfort occasionally on a December evening, it is an unusual summer that does not provide a scattering of days when the temperature rises to near or above 100°F (38°C). During exceptionally hot summers in the northern inland, shade temperatures rise to or above 100°F (38°C) on a few days. Summer afternoons hotter than 100°F (38°C) are frequent over the inland in the tropics; the most persistently hot area is inland from Port Hedland, western Australia, where at Marble Bar from October 1923 to April 1924, there were 160 consecutive days with temperatures rising to at least 100°F (38°C). The highest air temperature recorded in Australia (127.5°F) (53.0°C) was not at Marble Bar but at Cloncurry, Queensland.

The mean temperatures (Fahrenheit) of the hottest months for the capitals, with those of the coldest months in parentheses for comparison, are: Sidney 71.6 (53.3), Melbourne 67.7 (48.9), Brisbane 76.9 (58.6), and Darwin 85.3 (77.1). Australia's coldest regions are the highlands and tablelands of Tasmania and the southeast corner of the mainland, where the only regular winter snowfalls in Australia occur. In winter, temperatures here frequently fall below the freezing point.

Average Temperature—Sydney, Australia

	JAN	FEB	MAR	APR	MAY	JUN	JUL	AUG	SEP	OCT	NOV	DEC
(C)	22.2	22.1	21.0	18.4	15.3	13.0	12.0	13.0	15.3	18.4	19.5	21.3
(F)	72.0	71.8	70.0	65.1	59.5	55.4	53.6	55.4	59.5	65.1	67.1	70.3

Sunlight and Solar Heat Gain

Australia's fame as a land of sunshine is no legend. Throughout the year the average number of daily hours of sunshine for each capital city is: Sidney 6.7, Melbourne 5.7, Brisbane 7.5, and Darwin 8.4. The average number of daily hours of sunshine is considerably greater in the inland.

Rainfall

The greatest precipitation occurs on the north coast of Queensland (more than 160 inches) and in western Tasmania (140 inches). Parts of the eastern seaboard and coastal areas in the north receive more than 50 inches of rain a year, as do the Australian Alps in eastern Victoria and southeastern New South Wales and the northeastern highlands of Tasmania. A vast area of the interior, stretching from the far west of New South Wales and southwest Queensland to the western seaboard of western Australia, has less than 10 inches of rain a year. Between these regions of heavy and very low rainfall are the extensive areas that experience useful to good rains. The driest part of Australia is an area of about 180,000 square miles around Lake Eyre in South Australia, with a yearly rainfall average of about 5 inches.

The average rainfalls of the capital cities, with the average number of days in which rainfall occurs in parentheses, are: Sydney 47.71 inches (150 mm), Melbourne 25.95 inches (43 mm), Brisbane 44.68 inches (124 mm), and Darwin 60.70 inches (97 mm).

Landscape

In the north, mainly on the eastern seaboard, forests and vegetation are those of the moist tropics. Farther south, east of the great Dividing Range in particular, the vegetation varies from that of the moist, warm temperate zone to the mild, well-watered temperate zone. In the far southwest of the continent there are magnificent forests of hardwood. Inland, although there are fine belts of trees, the progressively drier climate restricts their growth to the river fringes, and there are large areas without trees.

Australia's long isolation as a land mass has resulted in a vegetation very different from that of the rest of the world. This was not always so. Fossil records reveal that in the pre-Cretaceous period, Australia's plant life conformed to the basic groups of other countries, indicating that in that time Australia had land connections with Asia.

About 50 million years ago, toward the close of the Cretaceous period, Australia's land links with northern countries disappeared, isolating the country and its plant and animal life from the rest of the world. The relatively arid conditions that came to prevail over the Australian continent intensified the struggle for existence and led to the development of a large range of plant life capable of withstanding harsh conditions and surviving in poor soils.

In the areas of forest and woodland in the extreme southwest of the continent and along the east coast in the foreland of the Great Dividing Range, with a growing period of over nine months per year, trees grow to heights of up to 200 feet (60 m). On the northeast coast the rainfall pattern permits the growth of vegetation throughout the year. In this area are found the various types of rain forest.

Toward the interior of the country, the pattern of tree cover varies in accordance with climatic conditions. Here the climate does not favor a dense growth of forest. Instead, there are areas of more open woodland with an undergrowth of shrubs and grass in which the trees grows to heights of around 65 feet (20 m).

A notable characteristic of Australian vegetation is the wealth of plant life commonly referred to as *wildflowers*. Australians use this term for any small, flowering plant growing naturally in the country-side. There are thousands of species, many of which are found throughout the continent, but each state has its own large range of endemic groups. They are seen at their best and in greatest variety on certain sandy plains, sandhills, plateau lands, and mountain slopes.

Hurricanes

Australian tropical cyclones are ranked based on a scale developed by the Australian forecasters for storms in their area of responsibility—between 90 and 160E. The sustained winds are based upon a ten-minute averaging period instead of the one-minute period used in the United States.

AUSTRALIAN SCALE	SUSTAINED WINDS (KM/HR)
1	63–90
2	91–125
3	126–165
4	166–225
5	>222

CHAPTER **4**

Southern California

INTRODUCTION

Southern California, although geographically north of the Caribbean region, bears many similarities to it. Both were invaded and settled at approximately the same time by the Spanish and other conquerors. The climate of Southern California throughout the year is relatively constant, cooled by northeast Pacific breezes, with temperatures between 70° and 80°F as early as late February being the norm. Average temperatures range from lows in the mid-40s in December and January to highs in the mid-80s in July and August. The region is sometimes invaded by cold arctic air blowing down from Canada. This requires occasional heating during the winter months, which is easily attained by passive solar heating techniques and the more common strategically placed fireplaces. Earthquakes are frequent, and occasional hurricanes blow in from the Pacific.

The climate of Southern California, like that of the Caribbean, is influenced by topography and by its proximity to the seashore. The region has many hills and valleys, with plush vegetation and remark-

North America.

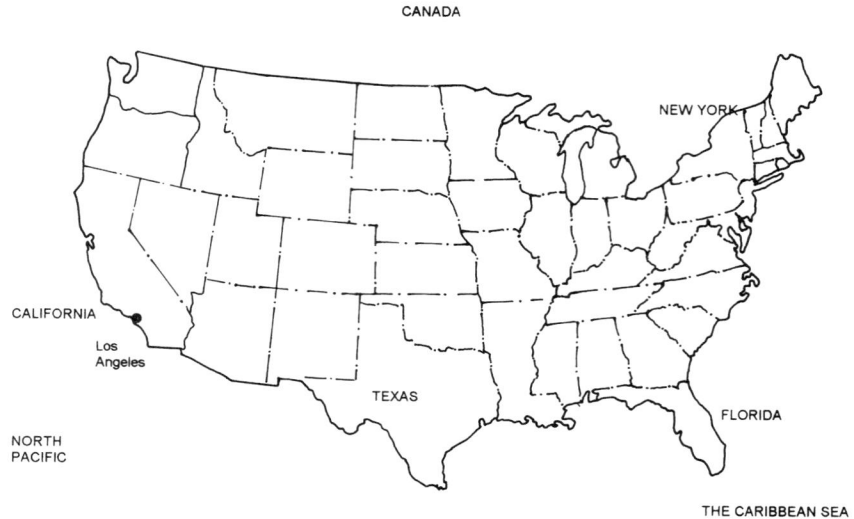

CANADA

NEW YORK

CALIFORNIA

Los
Angeles

TEXAS

FLORIDA

NORTH
PACIFIC

THE CARIBBEAN SEA

able views. American architecture there has benefited greatly from advances in technology. People in general, are now able to live in greater style than ever before, which means that they have become more and more dependent on energy (once relatively cheap) to maintain their comfort level and less on the passive natural means used by previous generations.

California.

Medford

San
Francisco

Los
Angeles

San
Diego

ARCHITECTURE AND CULTURE

Native American Architecture

The native inhabitants of the Los Angeles Basin, members of the Shoshonean language group (later given the tribal name of Gabrielino, from their association with the Spanish mission of that name), did not build monumental structures of stone or adobe like the Aztec and Mayan peoples, since the Southern California climate precluded the need for insulated shelters. The Gabrielino instead developed an efficient minimal architecture of domed, circular huts thatched with fern, tule (a large bulrush that grew in the marshes), or carrizo (a reedlike grass). Some huts were small; others were large enough to hold a sizable gathering. If these huts were located by the sea, doorways were placed seaward to avoid the cool north wind.

The natives lived in about 50 to 100 villages, each inhabited by 50 to 200 persons. In addition to the circular dwellings, a typical village had a number of sweathouses (small, semicircular, earth-covered structures used for cleansing and as a meeting place for adult males) and menstrual huts. Each village also had an oval, open-air enclosure called a *yuvar*, made with willows inserted wicker-fashion among willow stakes, decorated with eagle and raven feathers, skins, and flowers. Another building, similar in structure and design to the *yuvar*, was sometimes used for ceremonial instruction and practice.

The Spanish and Mexican Period

In 1542, half a century after Columbus discovered the New World, Juan Rodriguez Cabrillo sailed up its western coast and entered Santa Monica Bay. For more than 350 years, California was part of the Spanish Empire, with Mexico City, the capital of New Spain, located on the ruins of the Aztec city Tenochtitlan. During that period, California remained an unknown land of desert and mountains whose potential bounty was eventually realized by European settlers of the 18th century.

To maintain control of this vast country, Spain had to colonize the region. The immediate problem was: by whom? Mexico did not have enough able-bodied subjects to spare for the task, and the Spanish did not allow foreigners to settle in their colonies. The pope's response was to assign all of America and its inhabitants, except Brazil, to Spain on the condition that they be Christianized. So the Church and the state set out to convert the natives, train them in the ways of the Spanish, and teach them to be self-supporting citizens.

For fifty years the Spanish Franciscan missionaries established twenty-one missions stretching north to Sonoma. In addition, military garrisons were located in San Diego, Santa Barbara, Monterey, and San Francisco to guard the missions under their respective jurisdictions. The result was the imposition of an institution on an indigenous Indian culture different from the societies that the Spanish had encountered in Mexico and the Rio Grande Valley.

The influence of the Spanish mission on the Gabrielino culture played a major role in destroying their civilization. The Christianizing of the native peoples introduced domestic cattle and horses, new plants including citrus fruits, olives, figs, and grapes, cereals, and garden vegetables to support the missions. They were to be reared and grown by the mission Indians, supervised by the Franciscans.

Today Southern California bears little resemblance to its original semidesert landscape, having been transformed into a place of lush greenery and exotic species. The knowledge of irrigation brought by the Spanish enabled them to harness the intermittent streams, making water available for the various ranching communities that followed.

California Mission Architecture

Another principal effect of the missions on native culture was the eventual obliteration of indigenous architectural forms and their replacement by crude versions of the European buildings the missionaries knew, using whatever resources were available in California. Kurt Baer, in his study of California mission architecture, suggests that the decorative elements of the mission buildings were heavily influenced by the Moors through their 700-year occupation of Spain.

The Spanish in Mexico built upon the rich masonry architecture of the natives, creating fine monuments. In California, by contrast, the lack of resources and architectural skills on the part of both Indians and Spaniards tested their perseverance and ingenuity. The result was a plain architecture, with a few details in window arches or the curve of a wall parapet being the main symbols of the style.

The history of mission architecture has been described as "a series of stages in coming to terms with the limitations and potential of local materials" (Gleye, "The Architecture of Los Angeles," p. 16). In the first stage of their evolution, the missionaries had to compensate for the structural limitations of the local building materials. The first mission buildings in California were constructed of posts of pine or cypress set close together, plastered inside and out with clay, with an earthen roof. Walls were sometimes made of adobe, but roofs were often supported by forked wooden poles, relieving the adobe

Plaza Church 1822
El Pueblo de Los Angeles
State Historical Park
North of the Hollywood
Freeway on Main Street
Los Angeles, California

The plaza was the center of the Spanish pueblo and the center for worship for the small village.

from structural loads. The second stage of mission architecture utilized more adobe (stone where possible) as structural walls supported a roof of poles and rushes.

The earthen roof offered little protection to the soft adobe walls from the rain, which melted it into mud from which it came. Roofs made of reeds in the native style were vulnerable to fire. With this in mind, the missions were forced to develop a more durable roofing system, replacing older roofs in major buildings with fired brick roof tiles. Floors were usually of tamped earth covered with square brick tiles.

The most significant element of mission architecture, based on what architects used as its expression in reviving the style in the late 19th century, was the tower. The tower, which "reached toward heaven" and housed the bell that regulated each day's activities, tended to be massively designed in a series of setbacks and was capped by a small dome.

Pueblo Architecture

The building forms of some cities in the North American Spanish colonies were adapted from pre-Columbian native cultures. The Spanish architecture of northern New Mexico retained many visual qualities of indigenous Pueblo Indian architecture of the Rio Grande Basin, for example, though some structural elements were supplanted. The Spanish brought to the Los Angeles Basin a set of urban forms from more established colonies to the south and east. For the most part they rejected the architecture of the Gabrielino villages, with its twigs and branches, as unsuitable to express the architecture of the Spanish crown.

The first series of buildings were huts of chinked palisades, which were apparently replaced by more comfortable adobe homes. Mary Mooney describes the interior of an early adobe dwelling, whose thick walls were pierced with small openings to let in light.

> The small window had neither sash nor glass. The door often consisted of a dried hide hung over the opening. Oftener it was made of willow or elder branches laced together with thongs of leather or rabbit hide, and a leather string was used to fasten it on the inside. The table was a rude board, supported by notched stakes, stuck into the earth floor.
>
> (Mooney, p. 45)

Houses generally had flat roofs covered with an unprocessed asphalt material, which often melted and dripped off eaves in summer and leaked in thin places when it rained in winter. Pitched roofs of red tiles were known but were probably less common than modern restorations suggest. Clean-swept, hard-packed earth floors were the norm; tile floors were rarely used. Fireplaces for heating were also rare but in some houses were located in the kitchen. Most cooking, however, was performed outdoors.

Wood for home construction in the pueblo found its way to California from Boston as early as 1800. Finished lumber was brought in from the New England sawmills by ships until 1851, when a sawmill was opened by Mormons who had settled in San Bernardino. Pitched roofs covered with shakes began to replace the old flat roofs as wood became more plentiful. Walls were customarily finished inside and out with a fine white plaster of lime made in kilns in the San Fernando Valley. Ceilings in the better houses were of wood, with beams exposed, and often decorated with grooves. In lieu of a ceiling, houses with a pitched roof had a thin canvas stretching from wall to wall.

Queen Anne Style

Settlers from the Midwest came to Southern California in 1880, during the dying days of the Spanish Empire, entering a predominantly Mexican/Native American region. They brought a style of architecture already popular in San Francisco and the East—the American High Victorian architecture called *Queen Anne,* with its eastern variant. This style, once considered an exercise in architectural indulgence, has recently come back into favor, not only for its contrast to the veneered plainness of today's tract home but also because it, more than any other style, evolved to incorporate design techniques that responded to the climate and the natural surroundings. This style was a celebration of the craftsmanship that resulted from the careful application of the new machine technology to building construction.

**Russell House
1316 Carroll Ave
Westwood, California**

Most of the architectural decorations were mass-produced in shops by machines invented during this period and were available by catalog to any builder. The invention of the sewing machine, the electric light, and many other devices in rapid succession transformed American life from dependence on the traditions of handwork and living close to nature to dependence on large-scale technology.

While the Queen Anne style developed in the eastern United States as an expression of confidence in human potential, it became far from subdued in San Francisco and Los Angeles. There homes became more picturesque and complex, and expressed the freedom permitted by the climate and the attitude of the time. Houses were adorned with an array of gables (with their deep overhangs to shade the sometime intense sun), dormers, and high chimneys. Towers and turrets, sometimes hexagonal or square, with conical roofs, released hot unwanted air from the interior, which, when rising, would pull in and be replaced with the cooler outside breezes. The concrete blocks were reinforced with steel rods. Thus reinforced, they could be used for all purposes—for example, to span openings, as well as support weight and provide some resistance to light seismic forces and wind turbulence.

Inness House
1329 Carroll Avenue
Westwood, California

Exterior walls, usually of wood but occasionally of masonry (stone), acted as heat traps to absorb the daytime sun, and a grandiose porch, shaded sometimes by decorative slots with deep overhangs, would often wrap around the entire ground floor. Chimney construction became an exceptional art form; the brickwork of a chimney covered half of an exterior wall and rose in complex forms high above the roof. While some observers might find the decorative adornment of this period excessive by today's standards, the techniques of design and craftsmanship are worth revisiting. However, despite its popularity, the appeal of the Queen Anne style began to wane around 1890, due mainly to the lavish application of decorative forms and the fact that the style could not be further elaborated in any meaningful way. Especially with persons with conservative taste, the style became increasingly applied and related little to the surrounding and its occupants.

The California Bungalow

Prior to being settled by Anglo Americans, the Los Angeles Mexican dwelling consisted of mud walls with mud floors. The walls were whitewashed, and the ceiling looked like an old smokehouse. Some settlers quickly adapted the indigenous forms and materials but introduced their own styles into the new environment. Cooking was moved to an indoor fireplace. Architecturally, this transformation (the Anglicizing of the Mexican dwelling) resulted in what we call the Monterey Style.

While the evolution of the California bungalow is still being debated, it is believed to have grown out of the English arts and crafts movement and was the first style since the Monterey style that was truly indigenous to California. The style was partly a reaction against the excessive decoration and extravagance of the Queen Anne style and partly a western interaction between the natural environment and the culture. At first, the craftsman's technique was applied to the two-story American home imported from New England. Eventually it was applied to the bungalow, a single-story dwelling type that can be traced back to British India.

Historians also theorize that the California bungalow evolved from the barn. Many newcomers to Southern California around the turn of the 20th century were poor and built barns to live in while investing their money in their orchards. It is further theorized that

House
4715 Van Ness Avenue
Los Angeles, California

**Craftsman House
611 W 124th Street
Los Angeles, California**

the spindle work and Oriental details of the bungalow were of Japanese influence, originating at the Colombian Exposition in 1893 and the midwinter California Exposition in San Francisco in 1894. While the Japanese influence is apparent, that of the barn is difficult to trace. In any event the bungalow, with its simple, boxlike shape and informal floor plan, responded to the needs of the newcomers at that time. The main door opens directly into the living room, typical of modern design, rather than into the foyer, as in the Queen Anne home. The low house, with its shallow-pitched roof and broad overhangs to shade the building from the intense sun, is still a common feature of older Los Angeles streets. The covered front porch is usually large, deep, and raised to allow free circulation of air above and below. If California was the escape from the pressures of the East, the bungalow was its symbol, seeming to crouch cozily when the winds of the sea or mountain blows about and through it.

The Spanish Revival

Spanish architecture became the appropriate California tradition following the Panama–California Exposition. Soon Spanish forms were adopted as the "style" for building types and to entire urban districts to which it had not been previously applied. The institutionalization of the Spanish style reached its peak in Santa Barbara after the 1925 earthquake. Previously, there had been some interest in Spanish Revival forms in that city, but much construction had followed eastern architectural style. The earthquake allowed reconstruction according to a Spanish design plan, especially downtown, where a

Fox Westwood Village Theater   1931
961 Broxton Avenue
Westwood, California

The Fox Theater is essentially Spanish Colonial Revival with a modern twist.

Union Passenger Terminal   1939
800 North Alameda Street
California

The design combines Spanish and Moorish influences with the moderne styles of the 1930s.

stretch of State Street was redesigned with arcade storefront. One feature introduced by the Spanish Revival style that attempted to re-create the Mediterranean lifestyle was the interior courtyard. Exotic apartment complexes were built surrounding such courtyards, which were planted with exotic flora, often with fountains and pools. In the balmy Los Angeles climate the courtyard served as an exterior hall-way and patio, providing shade for occupants and buildings and act-ing as buffers for the wind, which would later filter through open windows and doors through the building.

The Transitional Period

The 1920s saw the continued rejection of historical icons and the embrace of the machine age for its architectural inspiration. In the 1930s residential architecture continued to look forward for its inspi-ration, but now to American colonial and English models. A Monterey Revival arose in those years as well, but it merely allowed architects to use an "Early California" look without perpetuating the Spanish forms. The architectural vision of the future city that was brought to completion in the 1920s represented what was perhaps the most creative period in Los Angeles architecture. Art Deco was one of the styles that flourished during the 1920s, utilizing sheet metal and copper panels that now adorn the exteriors of many buildings. This style was one of the high points of Los Angeles architecture. As the name implies, however, the style was primarily a decorative approach to design that relied primarily on the creative power of the designer.

Despite attempts by architects to reject the classical motifs by the 1930s, one could again see their influences and their incorporation into Art Deco. The style was eventually rejected and ridiculed as the modern movement began to dominate the architecture of the period, and by the 1940s Los Angeles had embraced the new style, becoming an important center of its early growth.

Modern Architecture

Modern architecture has its roots in the style of industrial buildings and the attempts by architects to transcend the constraints of traditional forms.

The story of the architectural transformation into modernism has been told at great length, but part of that story not well known is the role of Southern California. The modern movement is rooted largely in designs associated with engineering and technology. Southern California, however, had a unique precursor in the Spanish Revival movement—a movement that attempted not to reach out to modernity but to reach back to tradition. In the hands of an innovative designer, the Spanish Revival style expressed the same cleanliness and planes seen in the work of Louis Sullivan and, in particular, Frank Lloyd Wright. In 1923, Wright had discovered a structural system that provided a rich surface texture and suggested the pre-Columbian style: hollow, precast concrete blocks that were patterned or perforated, to provide coolness and shade. In most cases, the house was designed so that it seemed to grow out the ground in which it stood. It usually exuded hospitality and coziness, with its open yet shaded plan. It came to convey a lifestyle of living more or less in the open air for pleasure, a feature that the climate easily accommodated.

Richard J. Neutra, a Viennese architect born in 1892, emigrated to the United States in 1923, encountering what he called a "fantastic living culture of some yet unknown people." He worked briefly in Detroit and Chicago and in 1925 came to Los Angeles to work with Rudolph

**Landfair Apartment
1937
(Richard Neutra)
Southwest Corner of
Landfair Avenue and
Ophir Drive
California**

Schindler. Two years later he set up his own practice. While applying advanced technology to his designs, Neutra concentrated on transparency in his domestic architecture, which was achieved by planning interior-exterior merges. The site entered the house and vice versa. This vision reached maturity in designs such as that of the Kaufman house (1947) in Palm Springs, where the interior of the home is barely separated from the rugged mountains behind it by a single pane of glass. The Spanish Revival style of the 1920s in Los Angeles, with its patios and courtyards, was easily grafted onto the architecture of the modern movement. This facilitated the indoor-outdoor lifestyle nur-

**Kaufman House   1937
(Richard Neutra)
234 S. Hilgard Avenue
Westwood, California**

An example of Neutra's design in the international modern style. The house takes advantage of the sloping site with the living space open towards the garden and away from the street.

Reed House   1960
John Reed
21536 W. Rambla Vista
Malibu, California

tured by California's climate. The modern movement, with its freedom from antiquity, gave the architect the freedom he required to respond to his environment and facilitate the indoor-outdoor lifestyle nurtured by California's climate instead of being restricted by rules dictated by styles. The modern era saw numerous examples of buildings that embody design techniques for a tropical climate. Most were ingenious inventions for their time, with some features borrowed from earlier periods, such as the Spanish courtyard, with its fountains and pools. In 1977 Charles Moore and Ron Filson designed the Shelton house, which is set on a hillside of rich foliage, combining elements of the California ranch house and the formal villa. The Los Angeles hillside and climate lent themselves well to the modern designs of the 1920s and 1930s, as well as the post-and-beam architecture of the 1950s. The post-and-beam style allowed the building to cantilever from the slope, providing a commanding view of the city below and capturing the natural microclimate features at will.

CLIMATIC DATA

Southern California has one of the most consistent and predictable climates, with all elements intertwining, working together, and depending on each other to create the environment. Without the ocean breezes, the sunlight would be intolerable, and without the sunlight and imported water, virtually nothing would grow in the region. The summer dry period is also hot, imposing considerable stress on plants and animals. Because of Southern California's complex geography, its local climates include humid, moderately cool tropical coastal areas, highly seasonal and moist elevated areas, and extremely arid, hot desert areas. To most people, however, Southern California has only two seasons: wet and dry. In January, February, and March come the real rains: heavy, torrential, and soggy. The last rainfalls usually occur in April. Spring arrives with the last rainfall and ends with the first desert winds, which usually come in May and last for several days. The ocean breeze suddenly ceases as the hot, dry desert winds come whirling down the canyons and rush out across the valley. The desert winds often proceed the last rain of the season. By late May it is already fall in the hills. In late August the sea breeze dies, and once again the desert winds sweep across the land. As shown in the temperature table, this is the warmest period of the year. Hillside brush fires frequently occur, with devastating consequences. Toward the end of the summer one can see, as the novelist James M. Cain has observed, that "the naked earth shows through everything that grows on it."

Temperature

The average high temperatures in summer may be as low as 75°F (23°C) in the coastal and mountain zones and as high as 105°F (41°C) in the deserts. Generally, the maximums are higher the farther one is from the coast. The most extreme high temperatures range up to 125°F (52°C) in the low desert regions. The local climates range widely in their wintertime low temperatures. In the low desert regions, such as the Coachella and Imperial valleys, as well as in the cismontane regions, the temperature rarely drops much below freezing. In the high desert and the mountains, the winter minimum temperatures often go well below freezing. They are lower the higher the elevation, as low as −29°F (−29°C) at the highest points.

Average Temperature—Los Angeles, California

	JAN	FEB	MAR	APR	MAY	JUN	JUL	AUG	SEP	OCT	NOV	DEC
(C)	15.5	16.0	15.5	17.2	17.7	19.4	21.0	21.1	21.6	20.1	18.9	16.0
(F)	60.0	61.0	60.0	63.0	64.0	67.0	70.0	71.0	71.0	69.0	66.0	61.0

Average Temperature—San Diego, California

	JAN	FEB	MAR	APR	MAY	JUN	JUL	AUG	SEP	OCT	NOV	DEC
(C)	15.5	16.0	16.0	17.2	17.7	19.4	21.1	22.2	22.2	20.1	18.9	16.0
(F)	60.0	61.0	61.0	63.0	64.0	67.0	71.0	72.0	72.0	69.0	66.0	61.0

Rainfall

The average annual rainfall in regions of Southern California ranges from less than 2 inches (5 cm) in some desert areas to more than 50 inches (125 cm) in the higher mountain areas. In addition to the annual total, the seasonal distribution of precipitation in any form is important to vegetation. For most of Southern California, the vast majority of precipitation comes as rain in the winter months (November through April). The summer and fall are dry.

Average Rainfall—Los Angeles, California

	Jan	Feb	Mar	Apr	May	Jun	Jul	Aug	Sep	Oct	Nov	Dec
(mm)	73.6	60.1	50.8	20.3	2.5	0.0	0.0	2.5	5.0	7.6	35.6	40.6
(in.)	2.9	2.4	2.0	0.8	0.1	0.0	0.0	0.1	0.2	0.3	1.4	1.6

Average Rainfall—San Diego, California

	Jan	Feb	Mar	Apr	May	Jun	Jul	Aug	Sep	Oct	Nov	Dec
(mm)	55.8	40.6	48.3	20.3	5.0	2.5	2.5	2.5	5.0	10.0	27.9	35.6
(in.)	2.2	1.6	1.9	0.8	0.2	0.1	0.1	0.1	0.2	0.4	1.1	1.4

El Niño

El Niño, a recurring weather phenomenon, disrupts weather patterns and brings torrential rain and heavy mountain snow to California, especially to the southern part of the state. The southern United States from California to the Carolinas experiences wetter and stronger than usual Gulf of Mexico storms, resulting in massive flooding and landslides in the South and milder winters in the North.

El Niño refers to changes in the patterns of Pacific Ocean water temperatures and winds that affect the weather globally. Warm water heated by the tropical sun usually moves eastward from the western Pacific toward the coast of South America every three to seven years, with the warmest water and clusters of large thunderstorms moving to the central Pacific. When the warm water reaches the South American coast, it spreads north and south along the coast, creating the warmer than usual El Niño along the coast of Peru. The El Niño effect changes the size and location of the storms, which in turn alters the jet stream winds that steer storms. The altered tracks of these storms then disrupt normal patterns of wet and dry weather, not only in the Pacific but also in North and South America and as far away as Africa.

The 1982–83 El Niño caused more than $2 billion in damages from storms and flooding in the Pacific coast, Rocky Mountain, and Gulf Coast states. On the other hand, the warmer winters saved

$500 million in fuel bills, with the eastern United States experiencing the warmest winter in twenty-five years. In contrast, the 1976–77 El Niño brought droughts to California and one of the century's coldest winters to the Midwest and East.

Until 1982, forecasters were reluctant to predict in great detail when the next El Niño would occur and what it was likely to do. However, the costly 1982–83 experience prompted intense research into this event to determine the conditions leading up to it. Knowing the depth of the unusually warm water and the speed and directions of the underwater currents was helpful in tracking and predicting El Niño. The data analyzed now come from seventy buoys spread across the Pacific along both sides of the Equator. Warmer than usual ocean temperatures are a good indicator that El Niño is beginning. The 1997/98 El Niño developed very rapidly during April–May 1997 and reached strong intensity by June. Its magnitude and extent were comparable to the 1982/83 episode, which was the strongest El Niño of the century. The most recent El Niño includes abnormal patterns of rainfall and cloudiness over most of the global tropics, and nearly shut down the normal easterly winds. The primary impacts have been in the tropics and subtropics, and across the eastern South Pacific and central South America.

North America received its strongest El Niño impact during the winter and early spring 1998. The region experienced abnormally wet conditions due to increased storminess and onshore flows. (*USA Today,* Copyright © 1997, used with permission.)

Hurricanes

The frequency of storms along the Southern California coast appears to be cyclical. Between 1884 and 1893, historical records and shoreline maps indicate a simultaneous occurrence of high rainfall and unusually large storm waves. The same is true for the early 1940s, when waves up to 40 feet (12 m) in height were measured. Partly because of the cyclical nature of storm waves, the shoreline of California will erode or retreat in an erratic fashion. No meaningful rate of erosion can be determined because there can be as little as one year or as many as forty or more years between sudden and catastrophic retreats as the bluffs cave in. This is a very different pattern from that of barrier islands, which tend to beat a steady and predictable retreat.

In January 1983, the giant Pacific storms that struck California's beaches produced banner headlines across the country, as did smaller storms in 1979 and 1981. The 1983 storms were particularly newsworthy because the waves crashed into the living rooms of beach houses in Malibu.

Earthquakes

Several earthquakes with a magnitude of at least 5.0 on the Richter scale have struck Southern California from 1988 to 1998. The biggest quake was the Landers earthquake on June 28, 1992, measuring 7.3. It was the largest earthquake to hit Southern California since the Kern County earthquake of 1952, which measured 7.5. This quake was accompanied by three other sizable earthquakes plus tens of thousands of aftershocks, over a dozen of them measuring more than 5.0. The Big Bear earthquake was the second largest, measuring 6.4; it followed the Landers main shock by more than three hours. The third largest earthquake was the one that ultimately led to the Landers quake. It measured 6.1 and occurred on April 22, 1992. The Landers event also triggered the Mojave earthquakes, which occurred on July 11 of that year.

The years 1994–98 included several events, with at least two quakes a year with a magnitude of 5.0 or more. The Wheeler Ridge earthquake of May 27, 1993, had a magnitude of 5.2 and was the largest event in Southern California that year. The next largest earthquake was a Landers aftershock of magnitude 5, which occurred on August 20, 1993, near the original Landers epicenter. In 1994 the Northridge earthquake of January 17 was the largest, measuring 6.7. The Landers and Northridge aftershocks continued throughout 1994 and 1995—the largest, with a magnitude of 5.0, occurring on June 16, 1994. The Ridgecrest sequence began with a magnitude of 5.4 on August 17, 1995, and peaked with a magnitude of 5.8 on September 20.

The largest earthquake of 1996 was an aftershock of magnitude 5.2 that struck the Ridgecrest area on January 7. On November 27 the "seismic event of the month," the Coso main shock, struck, with a magnitude of 5.3. On March 18, 1997, the Calico earthquake struck, with a magnitude of 5.1. This was followed on April 26 and 27 by two quakes, which were Northridge aftershocks with magnitudes of 5.1 and 4.9, respectively. They occurred in the early morning, causing minor damage, and produced numerous aftershocks.

PART TWO

Climate and Design

CHAPTER 5

Climate and Associated Phenomena

TROPICAL CLIMATE: GENERAL CONSIDERATIONS

The climate of tropical regions on coastal plains is very enervating and in warmer seasons can be too hot for comfortable sleep at nights. The months of January to April are usually the most pleasant. In mountain areas, the conditions are generally pleasant most of the year and the atmosphere is fairly dry.

Our environment is a product of the variety of climates of the earth and the natural geology of the various regions. In our effort to control the environment, we modify and adapt it by our skills and intelligence, and in so doing produce an architecture and a landscape suited both to us and to the environment. The regions selected for analysis have two distinct climates: the hot-dry, tropical land climate and the hot-wet (humid) tropical climate. The hot-dry tropical lands lie between the two mean annual isotherms of 68°F (20°C), with vapor pressure below 25 millibar. The temperature in the hot season of the hot-dry tropics may reach 110°F (43.33°C). It usually drops at the rate of 3.5°F (2°C) for every 1,000-foot increase in altitude, and the vapor pressure is usually higher over land near large areas of water, where humidity is high due to wind and vegetation.

The hot-dry tropics have very high daytime temperatures of 80–130°F (26.67–54.44°C) in the summer months combined with strong sunlight reflecting unmercifully from light, dry, and sometimes parched earth. Due to the changing altitude of the sun, which in the winter may produce temperatures as low as 45°F (7.22°C) with shorter days, there is a great difference between summer and winter climate. The sky is usually cloudless and clear, with a deep blue glow at night, and the sunsets are one of the most spectacular events to behold. There is very little rain, low vapor pressure (7.5–20 millibar), and a relative humidity often below 50 percent). Flash storms occasionally occur in which where as much as 2 inches (50–80 mm) of rain may fall in an hour. Total rainfall is less than 10 inches (254 mm) spread over about thirty days per year and often leads to water shortage.

The hot-wet (humid) tropical climate is very different, characterized by high relative humidity (often 90 percent), heavy rainfall, and a year-round mean temperature of more than 64°F (17.77°C), sometimes reaching almost 100°F (37.78°C) in the hot seasons. The highland area usually varies greatly, as both the diurnal and annual temperature ranges are far less than those in the dry tropics.

Vegetation is usually dark green year round, with two wet seasons and rain concentrated in coastal areas. The glare is greater than in the torrid zones but may be duller when the sky is overcast. Wind speeds are generally low (tempered by the thick foliage) but may reach 80 mph in open areas, with violent squalls accompanying tropical thunderstorms. Fungus and termites are common. The proper response calls for protection from the rain and sun while allowing the air to move around both humans and buildings at will. Moving air helps to dry sweating skin and thus relieves the discomfort.

In the dry tropics, heavy shade internally, exclusion of intense glare, and dust protection are primary factors in the design and orientation of buildings. The humid zone requires shade externally by means of large overhangs and other devices that also give protection from driving rain so that the main walls of the building may be as open as possible to allow air movement through the building. The proper response to the climate depends not only on the above factors but also on health, clothing, acclimatization, and one's state of motion. In order to design for these conditions, an architect must understand the three ways in which the body can lose heat: by radiation, convection, and evaporation. Heat loss by radiation and convection takes place only when the air and the surroundings are below body temperature. Heat loss by evaporation takes place only if the air is dry enough to absorb further moisture. The rate of evaporation depends on the humidity of the air and the rate at which the air passes over the body. Cooling can be provided by a fan or wind if the air is below body temperature and not moisture saturated. Activities of daily living usually take place outside during the day and evening in the humid tropics when it is not raining. The climate thus dictates social customs that allow large areas of bare skin to be exposed.

The afternoon in the humid tropics is brief. The tendency in outlying rural districts where no electricity is available is to sleep during the hours of darkness. The day usually begins at sunrise. Safety in design is just as critical as human comfort, as the hazards of hurricane winds, floods, earthquakes, and lightning are frequent. The earth retains infrared radiation from the sun, some of which is absorbed by clouds and dust. It is rapidly dissipated at night due to the absence of clouds and the clarity of the air. This is of paramount importance in choosing building materials. Surfaces with high *thermal inertia* such as mud absorb and release heat far more slowly than those with low thermal inertia such as metal. As a result, in the tropics, surfaces that heat up fastest and are hottest during the day become cool more quickly at night.

Lightweight materials do very little to block heat penetration; therefore, the tropical Australian house is not effective in such hot dry as well as hot wet climatic areas. What makes existence bearable there is the verandah, which shades the walls and the interior from the intense heat.

In hot-dry regions, materials with high heat-storage capacity perform better because they take a long time to absorb most of the heat received during the day before passing it on to the inside surface of the building. Houses built with thick mud, brick, or concrete block walls are very cool during the day; at night, when the temperature drops, the inside rooms often remain too warm for comfort. The correct response is to open all the windows and doors to let the cool air in. In Jamaica, families simply go out and sit under a tree. In Australia they go into the *spinifex cool house,* an outbuilding constructed from clumps of spinifex grass fixed to a chicken wire enclosure that is continually sprayed with water.

Because of high humidity, good cross-ventilation is necessary so that people can feel the uninterrupted flow of a breeze across their bodies. The Australian house, however, does not allow this, as the rooms are usually positioned back to back or linked via an internal corridor (rather than placed alongside each other in a single long row). The Australian house tends to fare much better in warm, humid coastal regions because the outside air temperature generally remains the same during the day and night. Day temperatures in these regions are not as high as those in inland areas (due to the cooling effect of the wind), but the houses still tend to get pretty hot unless attention is paid to proper ventilation and shading devices.

The choice of materials in the humid zones (where the diurnal temperature range is small) is less affected by rapid temperature changes. In damp, humid climates, by contrast, the prevalence of insects and fungus growths are important factors. The sun casts a shadow on the buildings, varying with the position of the sun at different time during the day. By means of various instruments, (e.g., the heliodam), the degree of penetration has become definite and predictable, and the effectiveness of sunshade devices and the measurement of daytime lighting and reflection from adjacent surfaces may be determined. Building materials are subjected to expansion and contraction, depending on their temperature resulting from sudden storms or diurnal changes in the range of temperature. Cool permanent colors and smooth surfaces are preferred, and materials such as cement plaster, coral, and limestone are useful since their high plasticity and thermal inertia are valuable attributes. Paints and plastics in the dry tropics generally do not behave well and go through photochemical changes.

Tropical climates can be roughly defined as shown on page 101.

CLIMATE SUMMARY

Temperature

The tempo of life is slower in the tropics than in cooler climates; however, during the day, the temperature is probably seldom above skin temperature, even on coastal plains. A combination of high temperature and high humidity in built-up areas (particularly commercial ones) can be very unpleasant because of the lack of air movement due to breeze shadow.

Humidity

Relative humidity is high in coastal lowlands and unpleasant when the breeze drops or the location is in breeze shadow. The evaporation of moisture from the body in still air is consequently low, with much discomfort.

TROPICAL CLIMATES
Warm-wet to hot-wet (humid)

1. Equatorial lowlands, 7.5° north to 5° south of the Equator at or near sea level, close to the sea, lake or river basin (e.g., Java, Indonesia, and the whole coastal rain forest area).
2. Tropical inland trade wind coasts: Farther north and south, more seasonal, still equable and more sunny, warmer by day, cooler at night, humid but with cooling breezes. Note: Accra is more like (2) than (1) due to cool breezes (e.g., Jamaica and other Caribbean islands).

Intermediate—tropical Islands (cool to cold-wet)

Between 5° north and 15° south): Season due to latitude. (The season varies based on the island's location on the map.) Altitude above 1,000–2,000 feet will affect the quantity of rainfall (5° North latitude to 15° South latitude), creating dry and wet seasons.

Hot-dry (arid)

1. Low-latitude deserts or semideserts: Mainly inland, 20° to 25° north and south of the equator or, in extreme cases, 15° to 30° north and south; conditions are usually hot and arid.
2. Maritime conditions resemble those of hot, arid inlands but are less extreme, with very high humidity onshore. Offshore breezes sometimes slightly reduce the high humidity onshore.

Cool-dry (cooler uplands)

1. Equatorial: altitude makes air temperature cooler, especially at night (50–55°F—10–12.78°C); rainfall varies.
2. Tropical regions are more seasonal, with higher latitudes and more variable rainfall; in winter, temperatures may fall below 40°F (4.44°C); heating is required.

Rainfall

Rainfall can be high in all areas and a major concern to animal, pedestrian, and vehicle traffic flow. Dealing with surface runoff can be extremely difficult in towns, especially in built-up areas.

Flash storms may cause washouts and often the flooding of entire townships. The large number of gullies and the widespread evidence of soil erosion in Jamaica point to the danger of uncontrolled runoff.

Sunlight and Solar Heat Gain

The earth orbits around the sun annually while rotating about its axis (which is tilted 23⅓°) per hour. This results in our twenty-four-hour day, twelve-month year, the seasons, and the weather. In the Northern Hemisphere the sun is highest in the sky on June 21, the *summer solstice*—the longest sun day of the year. It is at its lowest point on December 21, the *winter solstice*—the shortest sun day. The midpoints of the solar altitude are on March 21 and September 21—the *equinoxes.* Solar installations are oriented to take advantage of various aspects of the solar year: winter/spring heating, summer/fall cooling, and so on.

As the earth rotates at the rate of 15° per hour, the sun appears to move through the sky proportionally. Depending on the latitude north or south of the Equator, each day the sun rises at a different angle from true south and attains a different altitude in the sky from horizontal south. Only on March 21 and September 21 each year, at the two equinoxes, will the solar arc and the times of sunrise and sunset be approximately the same. The shortest solar day occurs about December 21 (approximately a 120° angle on the ground and nine hours), and the longest occurs on June 21 (at 40° north latitude, approximately a 240° angle on the ground and fifteen hours).

Azimuth is the horizontal angle between the sun's bearing and a north-south line, as projected on a plane horizontal with the earth's surface. *Altitude* is the vertical angle between the sun's position in the sky and the horizontal plane of the earth at a given latitude.

Sky Condition

A hat or cool shade is often useful when exposed to sun or large sky areas, as the sun can be very bright when the sky is clear and the sunlight is intense. A combination of cumulus clouds and bright sunshine also leads to high brightness conditions.

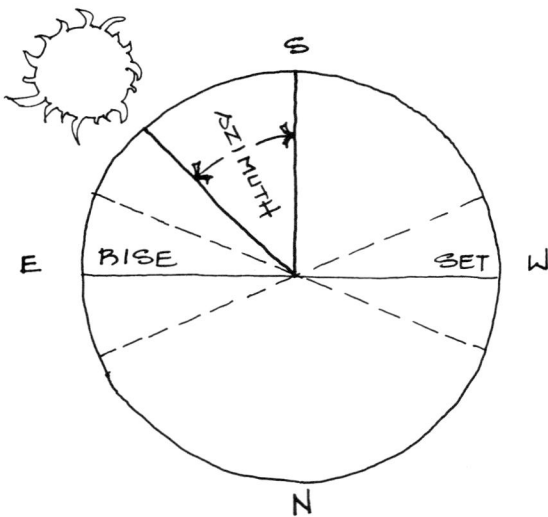

Diagram—azimuth.

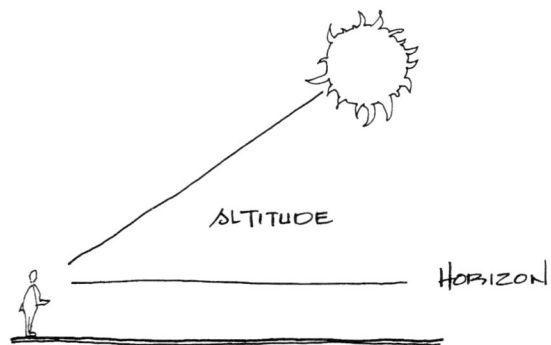

Diagram—altitude.

Ground Condition

Vegetation is luxuriant where rainfall is high. Much of the southern plains require irrigation and are dry and dusty during droughts. The soil is usually fairly dry, but a high water table is evident in most coastal ports and near marshlands.

Wind★

The buildings we design today tend to hold heat when we least want it; for some reason, we design them so that the outside air can't get inside to cool the buildings or their occupants. Before air conditioning was invented, many techniques were used to beat the heat, including taking advantage of natural air currents. The Greeks provided porticos around their temples for shade and breeze. The Arabs put scoops on their homes. The frontier American built dogtrots and porches so that they could sit in their rocking chairs and enjoy the cool breeze. The early Jamaican colonial style utilized large open, covered verandas, raised floors, large windows, and high ceilings in combination to provide an enjoyable, cool, shaded home.

These techniques are not lost to us. We simply stopped using them because we've become accustomed to air conditioning and cheap energy. We should remember that there are many times of the day and year when a natural breeze in the shade is all you need for comfort.

Breezes act according to the laws of nature, and one must understand certain scientific principles before one can determine accurately how to control air movement.

Global air pressure differences are caused principally by the sun warming some parts of the earth and those areas, in turn, warming the air, while other parts of the earth and air are not warmed as

★This section contains excerpts from an earlier article that appeared as "Letting Fresh Air Back into Buildings: The Evolving State of Natural Ventilation," by Benjamin Evans, FAIA, in *Architecture* (March 1989). © 1989 BPI Communications, Inc. Used with permission.

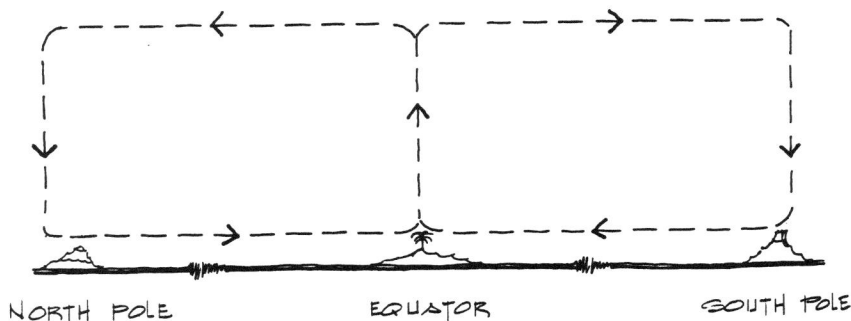

Diagram—global wind. (© 1989, BPI Communications, Inc. Used with permission)

much. The result is that the warmed air (higher pressure) tries to move toward the cooler air (lower pressure). The rotating motion of the earth also influences geographic air movements. As the earth spins, it pulls the air around with it, but the air does not keep up; slippage occurs. We have learned that air has mass and therefore is affected by gravity, and that it follows the law of inertia: mass once set in motion tends to continue in a straight line until its direction and speed are changed by some outside force.

All of these phenomena—pressure differences, inertia, and friction—tend to produce turbulence, so that air doesn't often move smoothly along a straight path. When two currents of air are traveling in opposite directions, they are always separated by a series of eddies because adjacent particles of air always move in the same direction.

Laboratory studies have shown that these eddies range from very large to microscopic, which cannot be seen with the naked eye. But at the scale of a single building, for ease of calculation in building design, we say that air moves in a fairly well-defined path.

Air motion through and around a microclimate influences everything. Constant wind affects humidity and ground moisture, moves soil and sand, and provides the potential for generation of electrical

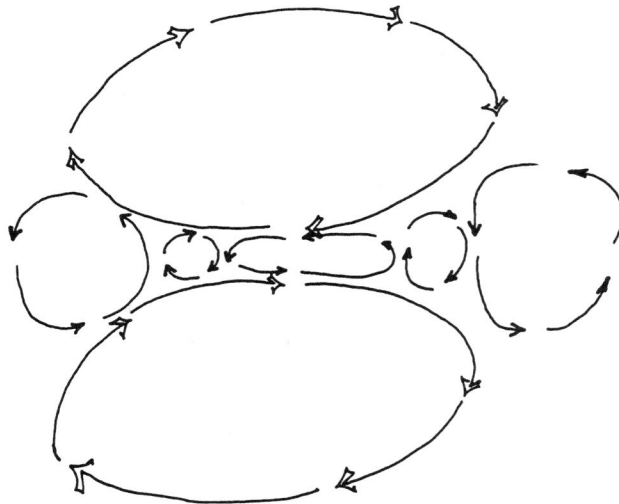

Diagram—local wind. (© 1989, BPI Communications, Inc. Used with permission)

Effects of wind on buildings. (© 1989, BPI Communications, Inc. Used with permission)

energy. Daily wind can be used to advantage for cooling and air exchanges. Coastal air movement provides welcome relief from the high humidity and temperatures of coastal lowlands. Wind is one of the climatological elements most affected by local influences.

Hurricanes

With average wind speeds of probably 125 mph and gusts of possibly 140 mph, hurricanes mainly cause economic damage, with some danger to life. Crops are often ruined, and poorly constructed houses, particularly on open sites, may be destroyed. There is always danger from pollution of water supplies and from floods near rivers, gullies, and coasts.

Earthquakes

The effects of earthquakes are mainly economic, although poorly constructed buildings can result in loss of life.

Associated Phenomena

Termites and Borers:
Termites and borers are of economic importance because they may result in constant replacement of vulnerable and important parts of the house. Their ravages may seriously weaken the hurricane resistance of a dwelling.

Fungi:
These can cause discoloration on surfaces, particularly those containing cement. They may be of economic importance in that some of them destroy paint, films, and softwoods.

Landscape

The key to comfortable survival is to balance all forces encountered in life while minimizing the effect of the natural elements. Proper balance involves using just enough of the climate and landscape to exist properly. Landscape and climate characteristics will dictate the most suitable setting, orientation form, materials, opening, and so on. Therefore, by understanding the landscape's characteristics—its potential, bearing capacity, land type, and so on, we can learn which type of structure is well suited for one area and not another.

Tropical land types vary from miles of white sand seashore areas and forests with a mainly tropical atmosphere to the hills and forests of mountainous areas with interlapping valleys and prairie land to the plains of the city.

Vegetation

The hierarchy of plant life offers an extensive collection for the landscape designer to draw from; more often than not, this is not done. The various plant types available can be used in very effective ways to modify the microclimate of a site. Grasses stabilize soil, retain rainfall, and harbor insects, birds, and small animals. Shrubs stabilize soil, make good ground cover and visual screens, and provide homes for many creatures. Deciduous trees provide summer shade and mulch for the ground, house birds, and channel breezes. Evergreens make good wind breaks and visual screens, as well as pleasant music when the wind blows.

Each land type, from desert to mountain to seashore, exhibits unique features of soil, weather, and terrain that can be generally categorized. It is clear that a type of structure well suited to one area and land type will probably not be suited to another without modification.

CHAPTER 6

Effect of Climate on Building Design

EFFECT OF TEMPERATURE ON DESIGN AND CONSTRUCTION

Temperature affects the design and construction employed, as it governs the measures to be taken to maintain comfort. Temperature can be reduced in a hot tropical climate by evaporative cooling through roof and walls. Cooling design strategies will be discussed in Part III of this book.

EFFECT OF HUMIDITY ON DESIGN AND CONSTRUCTION

When designing for a humid microclimate (over 60 percent relative humidity), it is prudent to allow air circulation, to consider dehumidifying, and to be aware of conditions causing walls to sweat and mold to grow. With its constant exposure to sea breezes blowing from across the Atlantic, Jamaica manages to dehumidify its environment naturally during most of the year, providing a comfortable environment. Lack of humidity or very dry air causes excessive evaporation of moisture, resulting in dry skin, nosebleeds, and inhibited plant growth.

EFFECT OF EARTHQUAKES ON DESIGN AND CONSTRUCTION

The results of earthquakes vary considerably, depending on the nature of the material constituting the ground surface at a particular point. Rocky areas, alluvial fan deposits, and sand spits are the principal types of ground surface found in Jamaica.

EFFECT OF HURRICANES ON DESIGN AND CONSTRUCTION

Roofs are particularly prone to destruction by high suction on their leeward side due to rapid air flow over the building or a combination of suction on top and pressure underneath the large overhangs so common in tropical areas. The effects of air pressure differences between the windward and leeward sides can also cause severe oscillations and result in collapse in the case of tall structures. The center of a cyclonic storm is at extremely low pressure, and if it hits a building that is particularly well sealed very quickly, the normal pressure inside the building can cause it to explode outward and collapse. Therefore, no building should be too airtight.

The rainfall associated with a tropical storm can be intense over a lengthy period, lasting for twelve to forty-eight hours and depositing as much as 3 to 12 inches (75 to 300 mm) of rain. In addition to the problem of flooding and the risk of landslides, water can seep into buildings, as well as damage foundations and materials. Certain materials and building techniques should be avoided. Walls of unburned earth or wattle and daub, clay mortar, and thatch or leaves in roofing, for example, are all susceptible to severe damage. In addition to considering the wind as a primary load together with the other primary loads (dead loads, live loads, etc.) when designing a building, many other precautionary measures must be used. These will now be discussed.

Foundation

Temperature: No effect on the design of the foundation.
Humidity: No effect on the design of the foundation.
Wind: No effect on the design of the foundation.

Sunlight: No effect on the design of the foundation.

Rainfall: A dished apron on ground (or a stone or gravel bed) under runoff eaves is desirable to protect footing; otherwise, there is little effect on the foundation.

Landscape: Stepped footing is employed for economic reasons.

Hurricane: Every part of the building should be anchored to every other adjacent part, especially through its foundation. Hurricane- and earthquake-resistant designs are interrelated.

Earthquake: A continuous spread foundation of reinforced concrete increases the resistance of a building to lateral forces. The first step in the design of a building, therefore, should be to provide a rigid foundation of reinforced concrete strongly tied together.

The increase in vertical pressure on the foundation resulting from the overturning moment due to horizontal earthquake forces should be considered. If the earthquake motion is from east to west, the overturning moment will increase the pressure on the foundation on the east side of the building. At the same time, the soil pressure on the west side will be correspondingly reduced. However, since the earthquake may come from any direction, static load pressure should not be reduced. There may also be a vertical acceleration due to the earth's motion that will increase or decrease the soil pressure, depending on whether the direction of the wave motion is up or down.

Building codes frequently permit an increase in the soil pressure for combined static and seismic loads. Ordinarily, the combined soil pressure should not exceed the normal allowable pressure plus $33\frac{1}{3}$ percent. In no case should the dimensions of footing be reduced below those required for static loads alone.

Many building codes require interconnection of footings as an important means of securing rigidity and a "moving together" of all units in the structure. Interconnected footings are easily provided at little added expense if reinforced concrete is used. The foundation tie can be either separated struts or a solid slab.

If struts are used, they should completely tie all parts of the foundation in two directions approximately at right angles to each other. Each member should be capable of transmitting both tension and compression of at least 10 percent of the total vertical load carried by the heaviest of the connected footings.

If a reinforced concrete slab is used, building codes require the thickness to be at least $\frac{1}{48}$th of the clear distance between the connected foundations but not less than 6 inches.

Floor Slab

Temperature: Slab-on-grade construction provides for ground temperature heat exchange.

Humidity: No effect on the design of the floor slab.

Wind: No effect on the design of the floor slab.

Sunlight: No effect on the design of the floor slab.

Rainfall: Low-lying areas prone to flooding should be avoided; otherwise, elevated floor slabs are most suitable.

Landscape: Economical to have slab stepped with slope, thus eliminating excessive excavation or filling.

Hurricane: In general, exposed, elevated sites, river mouths, and gully beds should be avoided. If areas are prone to flooding, an elevated floor slab on poles is best. Otherwise, in high land areas, a reinforced concrete slab is preferred for hurricane conditioning.

Earthquake: For lateral earthquake forces to be transmitted to the foundation of a building, these forces should be distributed to vertical members capable of transferring them down. This is accomplished by reinforced concrete walls that act as very deep, stiff vertical girders or by rigid frames consisting of columns and beams.

The floors serve as very rigid horizontal girders when constructed of concrete, and they distribute to walls and frames the lateral forces due to dead load.

Concrete floors having relatively small openings, and those designed for static loads possess adequate strength to function as distributing diaphragms.

Building inspections show that cracks occur in floors at the corners, indicating a concentration of stress. It is therefore important that the corners be thoroughly reinforced. Floors designed for static loads are generally adequate to resist earthquake forces.

Large openings in the floor weaken the slab and cause a concentration of stress. At such places, an amount of reinforcement at least equivalent to that interrupted by the opening should be located as close to the side of the holes as possible without crowding.

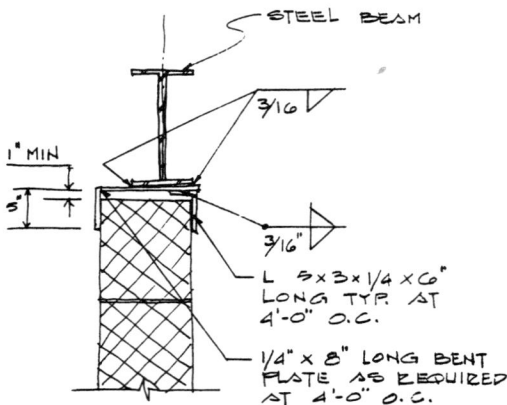

Detail 5.

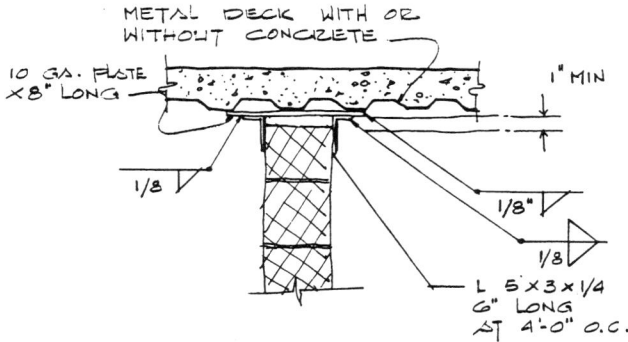

Detail 6.

Walls

Temperature: Heavy construction (blocks and concrete) reduces daily ranges of fluctuation about the average. The rise and fall of internal temperature does not immediately follow the changes outdoors due to the thermal capacity effect of these materials.

Humidity: Walls by themselves have no effect on humidity, except when incorporated with strategically placed openings to promote free air movement.

Wind: Walls, while designed to limit the intake of strong breezes, should also be provided with adequate openings as inlets and outlets to obtain maximum air movements for building occupants. Walls should be sturdy enough to withstand daily winds of up to 21 mph. Orientation for breeze requirements conflicts with sunlight requirements.

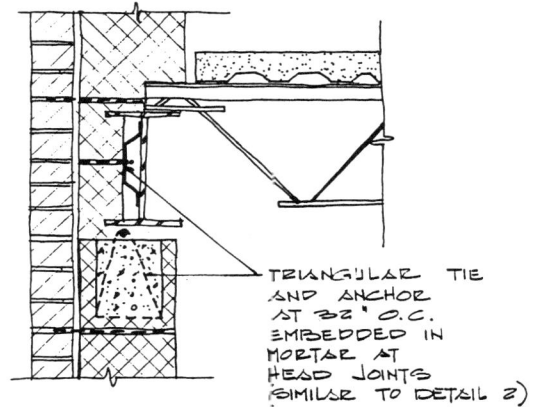

Detail 7.

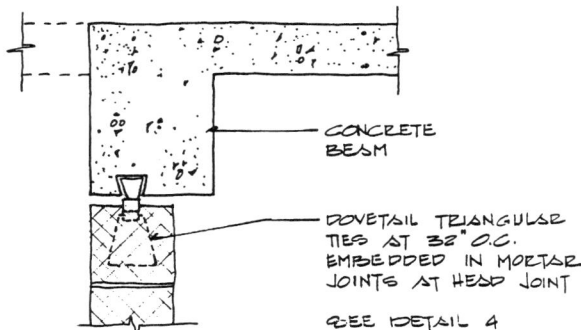

Detail 8.

Sun: Solar gain through exterior walls should be minimized where appropriate through various shading devices designed as part of the structure or through selected vegetation. Orientation of walls with the long sides facing north and south for limited sun exposure conflict with breeze requirements.

Rainfall: There is special danger of erosion around the feet of walls, especially those water collected from a pitched-roof overhang. The splashback from the ground carries up earth particles and may quickly spoil external decorative treatments. Aprons on the ground under runoff eaves are desirable to protect the wall base.

Landscape: No effect on the design of walls.

Hurricane: Reinforced walls have proven most resistant to hurricane effects.

Earthquake: Earthquake- and hurricane-resistant designs are interrelated. A bearing wall should be designed for a lateral

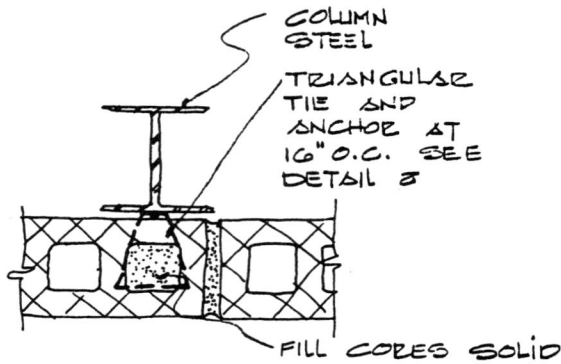

Detail 1.

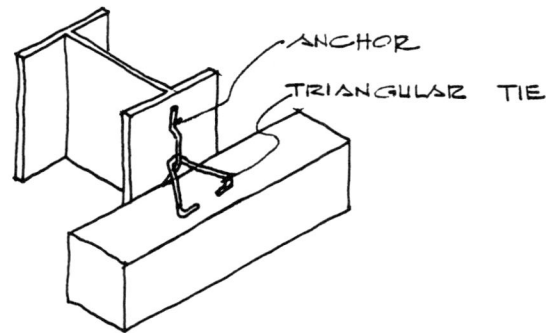

Detail 2.

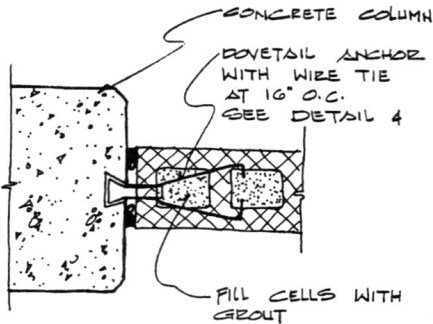

Detail 3.

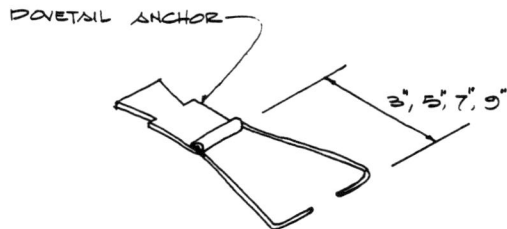

Detail 4.

force normal to its surface. Although a wall is generally supported laterally on four sides, it is ordinarily designed to carry horizontal loads over the shortest span, and in buildings this is usually the vertical direction. It is also important to provide adequate reinforcement at right angles to the main reinforcement in order to resist volume change stresses and to ensure unity of action.

Unless they are designed as cantilever walls, masonry walls must be laterally supported or braced at certain intervals. Lateral support may be furnished by either vertical or horizontal elements or both. The distance between lateral supports depends upon the type of construction (i.e., reinforced, partially reinforced, nonreinforced), the wall thickness, and the magnitude of lateral and/or vertical loads. When the limiting distance is measured horizontally, vertical supports may be pilasters, cross walls, or columns. The NCMA publication *Architectural and Engineering Concrete Masonry Details for Building Construction* shows commonly used connections for reinforced and nonreinforced concrete masonry walls.

Opening

Temperature: Generally, openings should be oriented to the north and south to limit the effect of direct sunlight. If openings are on the east and west walls, fixed vertical louvers are preferred where sun shading can be controlled. Excessive openings oriented to direct sunlight can greatly affect the internal temperature of the buildings.

Humidity: Free air movement, which is essential to alleviate discomfort, can be promoted by carefully spaced openings. Openings are preferably louvered for control. Orientation to catch breezes is an important design requirement.

Wind: In general, buildings should be sited and openings designed to obtain maximum air movement from prevailing breezes, generally blowing across the site from the northeast.

Sunlight: On seacoasts reflected light is most comfortable, and in mountain areas windows can be smaller or specially designed to eliminate glare from large sky areas. Generally, a north-south orientation is preferred to minimize glare from direct sunlight.

Rainfall: Rainfall has very little effect on the design of openings. Intense sunshine provides almost immediate evaporation from walls, ledges, and roofs. In general, proper construction and careful window selection is the best approach. Louvers can be adjusted to block angled rainfall while allowing some natural ventilation to enter.

Hurricane: Openings should be designed to shut tightly during a hurricane.

Earthquake: Lintels and beams across openings should be provided to take the effect of stress loads accompanying earthquakes. Open-front buildings, such as stores, garages, and markets lack structural bracing and often suffer severely in earthquakes. The front walls of such buildings and the interior cross frames, consisting of beams and their supporting columns, should be designed as rigid concrete frames that depend on the rigidity of their joints for stability.

Roof

Temperature: An unceiled roof with a highly reflective upper surface is desirable. Providing ceiling space in well-ventilated pitched roofs has little effect on internal temperature. Heavy roof construction reduces the daily temperature fluctuation, as the rise and fall of temperature do not immediately follow changes outdoors due to the thermal capacity effect of these materials. Roof spray may be incorporated to reduce the temperature by 40 to 50°F. Venting of the underside of the roof allows heat dissipation to the outside, eliminating heat buildup. Here a double-roof construction, providing free movement of air through the two layers, is desirable.

Humidity: Free air movement is essential to alleviate discomfort in buildings by day and during most of the year by night. Temperature and humidity designs are interrelated.

Wind: Roof openings should be designed to promote maximum air movement.

Sunlight: Glare from reflective metal surfaces, particularly sheet aluminum roofs, may prove troublesome (near airports). Shielding from low-angle sun on the open side is a problem. Concrete roofs need shading or treatment with a reflective surface and must be carefully designed to mitigate the effect of thermal stress.

Rainfall: Water for drinking is often collected from aluminum sheets or concrete roofs in rural areas where water supplies are short. Runoff from pitched roofs causes erosion around the feet of walls. Sheet roofs need good laps and good ridge flashing and, in common with bitumen felt, should be laid to steeper falls than in temperate climates.

CHAPTER 7

Conceptual Design Approaches

URBAN DESIGN AND CLIMATE

Climate is one aspect of planning that provides answers not available any other way. We know that, to some extent, cities create their own climates in response to how we alter the landscape. Studies show that when a landscape of plant and soil gives way to one of brick and concrete, the local climate changes along with the scenery. Understanding how this happens can help us to take control of the process. Designing subdivisions to create the best possible urban microclimate will result in

- A more comfortable environment
- Less energy needed for indoor comfort
- Money saved
- Emissions of greenhouse gases reduced

There are several advantages to including climate expertise and climate analysis in the design process. One is that the full potential of solar energy is investigated and realized. Other advantages include

- Air drainage patterns carrying pollutants away from residential areas
- City dwellers enjoying improved climate comfort
- Choosing the site of a new town to lessen the danger from natural hazards

In the climatically optimum city, the thermal comfort and even the health of some city dwellers improves. Less energy is needed for indoor temperature control. Peak power demand and peak storm water runoff are reduced, reducing the cost of city infrastructure.

CLIMATIC FACTORS IN DESIGN

The process by which architectural design is developed in response to specific climatic requirements was named *bioclimatic design* by the Olgyay brothers. Victor and Aladar Olgyay (in the early 1950s) were the first to give a well-defined concept of relating coincident temperature and humidity conditions to climate control and comfort in building design. Data on ambient climate conditions give the designer an accurate representation of the potential effect of the building envelope, as well as other environmental control strategies for achieving human comfort in buildings. By utilizing the natural effects of sun, wind, and nighttime cooling, design strategies can be identified. When these are insufficient, appropriate mechanical equipment may be selected.

Human comfort varies from culture to culture and from individual to individual as a function of one's physical condition, activity, or lack of it. For the tropical regions, where temperature averages 76 to 82°F throughout the year, comfort zones of higher temperature are permitted, corresponding to a dry bulb temperature of 88°F, with relative humidity ranging from 35 to 75 provided by the cooling effect of prevailing breezes. A building in the tropics differs from one in the temperate zone and can even differ in the same area where there are various influences on the microclimate. These changes should be recognized in the design and construction of buildings. For example, the air temperature in an urban area can be as much as 96°F higher than that in the surrounding countryside, with a relative humidity 5 to 10 percent lower.

Some of the factors to be considered when designing with the climate in mind are the following:

In a hot, dry climate: Sun protection is essential.

- Provide shade and pale surfaces to reflect the sun's radiation.
- Reduce glare and heat reflected from pale surfaces by providing shading from eaves, verandahs, and vegetation. (Trees are nature's own evaporative coolers—perfect for the dry climate if the water supply permits their growth. Trees also filter blowing dust from the air.)

In a warm, humid climate: Air movement is needed to keep us comfortable.

- Orient streets and buildings to catch the breezes.
- A mixture of building heights promotes ventilation and uses one part of the building to shade an adjacent part from the sun's rays.
- Vegetation must not impede air movement. Trees with branches far from the ground such as palms are ideal.
- Permeable surfaces are needed to reduce urban storm water runoff, as rainfall may be heavy.

In a temperate climate: Usually summer is too hot and winter is too cold. The wind direction usually changes with the season.

- Choose a street layout that blocks the winter wind yet allows cooling summer breezes to move through the city.

In cooler parts of the temperate zone or on exposed sites:

- Maximize wind protections (tree shelter belts, closely spaced buildings of constant height, main streets perpendicular to the prevailing wind).

STRATEGIES OF CLIMATE CONTROL

The building envelope controls heat exchange between the interior and exterior environments. The building envelope for a tropical climate should act to modify the exterior climate to create a new interior microclimate zone. The fundamental control options for the tropics are (1) excluding or, on rare occasions, (2) admitting heat gain from external energy sources and (3) rejecting or (4) containing heat present in the interior. Tropical microclimate zones consist of three basic zones based upon the geographical region: the internal mountain system, the limestone plateaus and hills, and the coastal plains and valleys. Each of these three zones, while having distinct similarities, requires a different approach based on the zone's influence on buildings and their design.

Most of the manifestations of control are static (e.g., insulation, orientation, glazing). Some, however, are dynamic. These include operable window sashes, movable window insulation, and a variety of adjustable sun-shading devices.

Ventilation Strategies★

Two primary strategies can be used for ventilating buildings. The suitability of each is related to the humidity of the climatic zone. We can label these strategies *continual venting* and *nighttime venting*.

Let's assume that we have a gentle breeze blowing along the earth's surface, moving from a high-pressure air mass over in the next county to a lower-pressure air mass somewhere down the road. On striking a solid object—a simple cube-shaped building, for instance—air movement is interrupted. As the air piles up in front (upwind) of the object, its pressure increases until it is forced over and around the object, creating a lower-pressure area behind it (downwind). Air in this lower-pressure area is eddying and moving slowly back upwind toward the solid object. This protected area is sometimes called the *wind shadow*.

Since air moves from higher-pressure to lower-pressure areas, it makes sense to locate a building's breeze inlet adjacent to the higher-pressure area and its breeze outlet adjacent to the lower-pressure area. To determine the best place for inlets and outlets, therefore, we need to

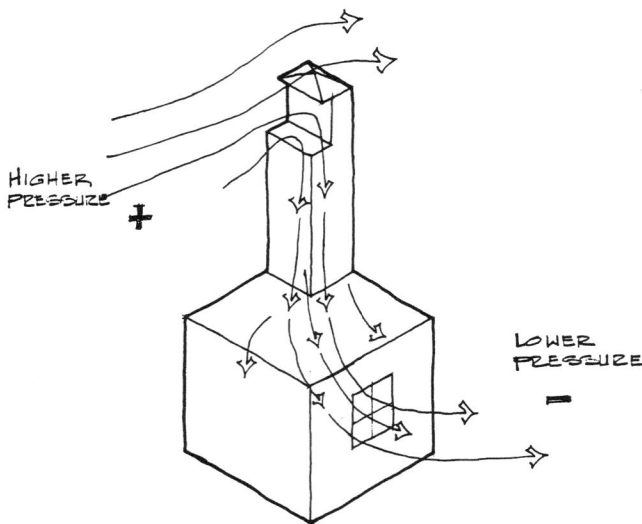

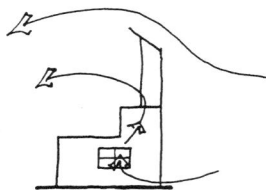

Wind scope (© 1989, BPI Communications, Inc. Used with permission)

*This section contains excerpts from an earlier article that appeared as "Letting Fresh Air Back into Buildings: The Evolving State of Natural Ventilation, by Benjamin Evans, FAIA, in *Architecture* (March 1989). © 1989 BPI Communications, Inc. Used with permission.

have some idea of where the high and low pressure will occur on the building's surfaces. For a building with a simple cube shape, the windward face of the is under positive pressure, relative to ambient air pressure, and the top, back, and sides are under negative pressure. Thus, it is easy to see that an inlet on the windward face and an outlet on any of the other surfaces will produce cross-ventilation.

Everyone knows that hot air rises. This does not contradict the statement that air is moved by pressure differences. As the temperature of a body of air rises, the air pressure differences cause it to flow toward a lower-pressure area, usually higher up. These *stack-effect* air currents are useful for exhausting unwanted air, such as the air that might collect under a skylight or next to the ceiling. They are particularly effective at night, when the cooler night air can be brought in to carry to the outside the heat absorbed by buildings during the day. However, they provide little evaporation because they do not move fast enough and usually do not pass through the living zone (where people are found).

Stack-effect ventilation usually allows prevailing breezes to overcome the effect of air movement caused by thermal differences. Even in areas where considerable process heat is emitted in the interior, mild cross-ventilation will overcome the stack effect and carry the heat out via the breeze. So a stack effect can work in conjunction with cross-ventilation.

In some Middle East countries, *wind scoops* have been used for hundreds of years to induce natural ventilation. These scoops rise above the roofs of houses to create pressure areas that pull the air into downstairs rooms, either down the scoop when the wind blows from one direction or into the windows and out of the wind scoop when the wind is from the opposite direction. Wind scoops do not push or force the air down into the building. The air movement into the interior is created by pressure differences caused by wind blowing over the wind scoop and the building.

A similar type of construction used in the Middle East to induce natural air flow is the *venting tower*. This tower rises above the building's roof to interrupt the wind and create a low-pressure area, regardless of wind direction. The low pressure over the venting tower pulls air into the building from the higher-pressure area below. This system requires manual opening of windows toward the high-pressure area.

Aids for Cooling

Wind catchers or wind towers can be found in hot areas ranging from Pakistan through the Gulf States to Egypt and North Africa. Although the form and details may vary from

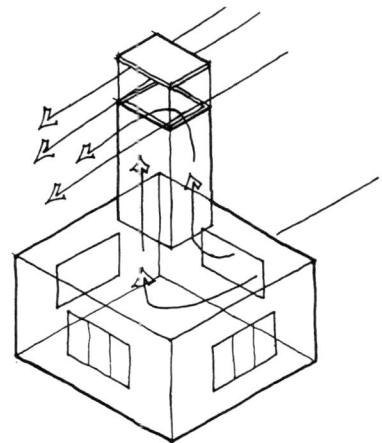

Venting tower. (© 1989, BPI Communications, Inc. Used with permission)

region to region, the basic principles of catching unobstructed higher-level breezes remain the same. In some places the catchers are unidirectional and oriented to catch the favorable breezes, while in other places, pivoted scoops and multidirectional towers utilize winds from any direction. In the courtyard houses of Iraq, for example, a series of wind catchers on the roof provide natural ventilation for a basement room where the residents normally take their summer afternoon nap. Each catchers is connected to the basement by a duct located between the two skins of an internal party wall that is cooled during the night by natural through ventilation. Because the party wall receives no direct solar radiation and because of its thickness, its surfaces remain at a lower temperature than the rest of the interior throughout the day. The incoming air is cooled by conduction when it comes into contact with the cold inner surfaces of the duct walls, and its relative humidity is increased as it passes over porous water jugs just before being discharged into the basement. After passing through the basement, the air flows into the courtyard, helping to ventilate this area during the daytime.

The same principle is used in the Pantheon of Rome. The round opening of the crown of the dome allows the low pressure created above the dome by prevailing breezes, regardless of direction, to draw fresh air into the interior through the doors on the exterior.

However it is achieved, cross-ventilation is not a matter of filling a building with air; rather, it is achieved by moving air through the building. You can't put water into a bottle that is already full unless you pour out the old water or put a hole in the other end so that the bottle can empty itself while you pour the fresh water in. The same is true of buildings and wind. For cross-ventilation, air needs a way in and a way out. This requires judicious use of outlets as well as inlets.

If we punch a hole through the building from the windward side to the downwind side, some air would move through this hole from the high-pressure upwind side to the low-pressure downwind side rather than going all the way around the building. This is what we

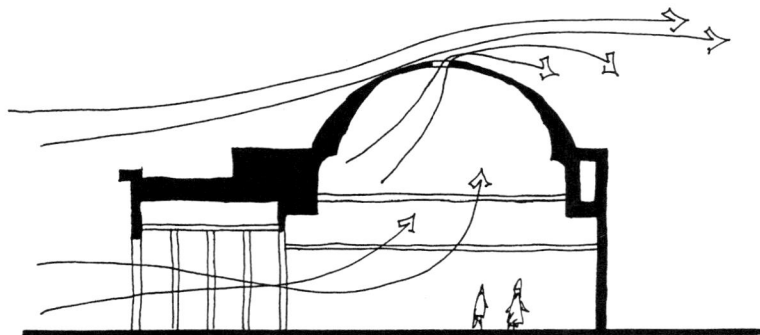

Pantheon of Rome. (© 1989, BPI Communications, Inc. Used with permission)

mean by cross-ventilation. It is the fundamental process by which air is moved through a building.

The principle that air flows from high pressure to low pressure helps us analyze airflow patterns and create new ones. This figure shows a building oriented so that wind approaches from a blind side (along with no windward inlet). Obviously, there will not be much air movement inside the building even when the windows on the ends of the building are wide open. There will be high pressure on the upwind side, low pressure on the downwind side, and low-pressure areas at both ends.

To move the air through the windows from one end of the building to the other, we need to create a new high-pressure area at the outlet. The solution is to attach a windbreak (see figure) that will create a high-pressure area immediately in front of it (at one end of the building). Another windbreak at the opposite end of the building toward the downwind side will further reduce the low-pressure area there, drawing the air from one end of the building to the other or crossways to the prevailing breezes. This solution will probably not create an ideal interior environment, but it will be an improvement.

Windscreens, like windbreaks, block the wind. Screens work better than a nonpermeable barrier. A solid fence provides less protection than a screen or fence with some holes. Wind speed in the

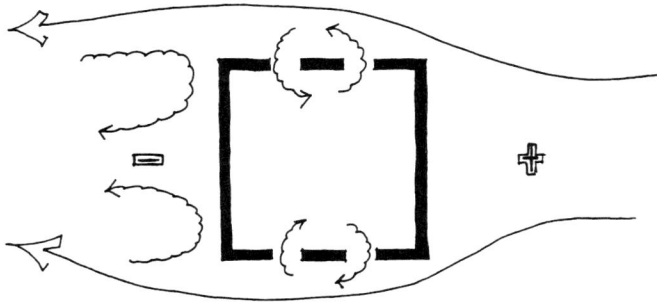

Cross-ventilation. (© 1989, BPI Communications, Inc. Used with permission)

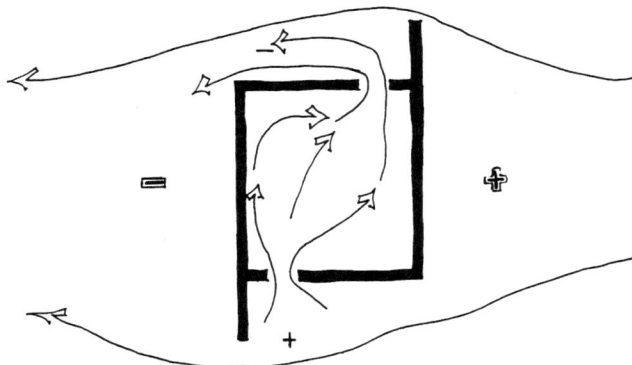

Cross-ventilation. (© 1989, BPI Communications, Inc. Used with permission)

(a)   PARTITION

(b)

(c)

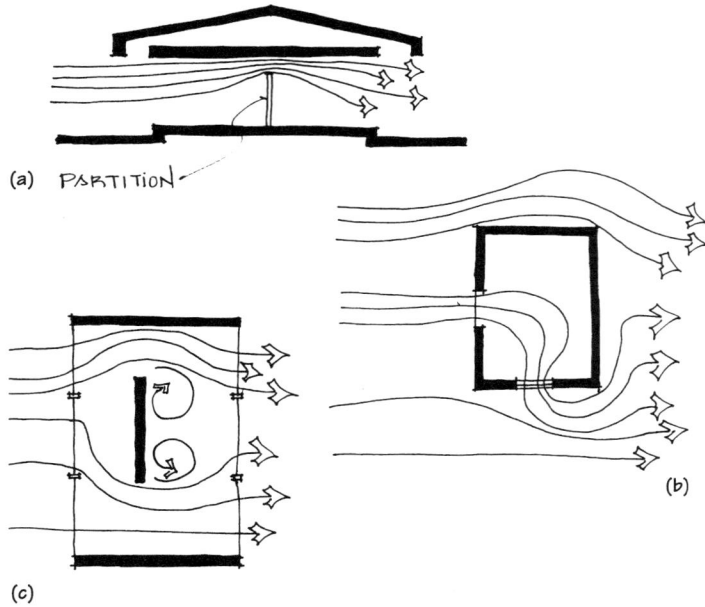

Ventilation: effect of openings on air current. (a) Partition; (b) air speed reduced by the "dog-leg" effect; (c) solid walls or a partition will create pockets of still air; (d) high-pressure area: pileup of air. (Fry, Maxwell and Drew, Jane, 1982, *Tropical Architecture in the Dry and Humid Zones,* 2nd edition, Krieger Publishing Co., Malabar Florida)

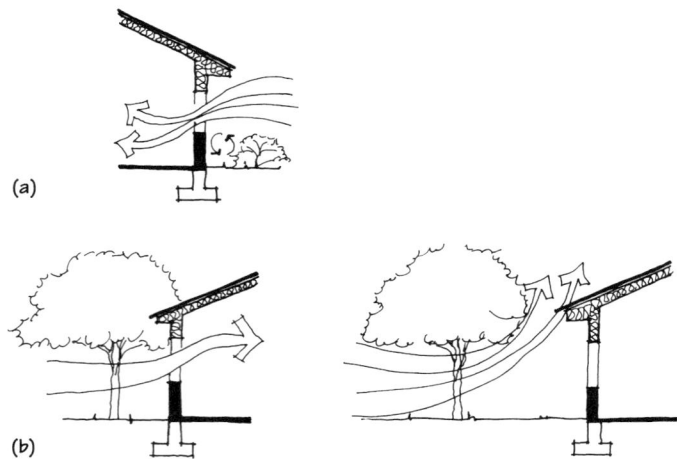

(d)

Wind Channeling. (a) Shrubs planted outside window will deflect the air downward; (b) Trees planted outside window will deflect the air stream upward.   (Watson D.: *Climatic Design* (1983), Reproduced with permission of the McGraw-Hill Companies)

(a)

(b)

wind shadow is slower behind a perforated screen than behind a solid fence. Wind speed is expressed as a percentage of the uninterrupted wind speed.

Once air enters a building, it keeps flowing until it hits something. It is easy to see how walls and doors force the air in one direction and then another. A breeze does not necessarily move directly from the inlet to the outlet except in special cases. So the pattern of an incoming breeze is not always affected by the location of the outlet.

The size of an opening does have an effect. Air speed is important in cooling. The faster the air moves, the more moisture and heat it will remove from the body by evaporation.

In very humid regions, comfort by natural means is attainable only with constant movement of air across the skin. In such regions, the diurnal temperature range is small owing to the suppression of thermal radiation to the sky by a humid atmosphere; the greatest thermal advantage in design is obtained with the use of lightweight building shells that cool off quickly at night. Daytime temperature control is maintained by ventilation, both for dissipation of solar heat absorbed by the building's shell and for body cooling. In extreme cases, the best structure is no structure at all except for a canopy to provide shade. In practice, elevated structures, roof ventilators, and wind-catching verandas are found as both traditional and contemporary elements of humid-region ventilation design.

Evaporative Cooling

Evaporative cooling can be achieved either through roof sprays and ponding or by extracting heat from the building through an evaporative treatment. In order to achieve the latter, the interior must be coupled with a highly conductive roof structure.

Warm air passing over water evaporates the water, and as a significant amount of heat is absorbed in the process, the air is cooled. The evaporated water is retained in the air, increasing its humidity. For this reason, evaporative coolers can be used only in relatively dry

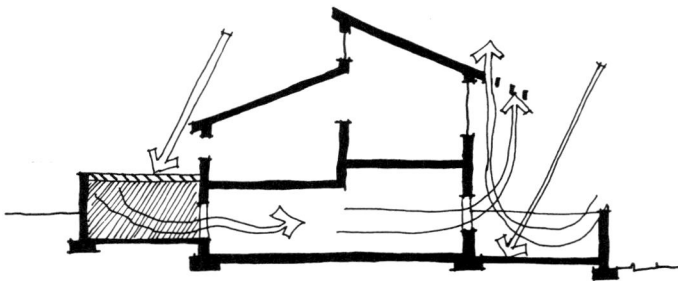

Evaporative cooling through courtyards. (Watson, D.: *Climatic Design* (1983), Reproduced with permission of the McGraw-Hill Companies)

climates, and are found in deserts, composite zones, and Mediterranean zones. These coolers are based on the evaporation of a thin film of water on a carrier over or through which air is passed. The simplest system is a wooden frame across which open-weave matting of vegetable fiber is stretched. When hung in front of windows in the path of the natural air flow and kept damp, the matting humidifies and cools the air, as well as filtering out dust. Another simple system entails the use of large, porous earthenware pots filled with water that allow air to seep through the walls of the pot, moistening the outside and cooling the passing air as it evaporates. Wind catchers, with beds of wet charcoal over which the air passes before entering the room, are sometimes used. The same principle can be used by channeling breezes over pools or water sprays before they enter building to ensure that the cooled and humidified air enters the building; the pool should be contained between walls on two or, preferably, three sides. A spray pond is more effective than a still pool of the same size and has the additional advantage that it not only cools the air but also "washes" it; the water droplets stick to dust particles in the air, removing them from suspension.

Thermal Transmission

Comfort may call for opening to or shielding from the wind at various times. Sheltered, outside-activity areas insulated from associated noise and reduction of heat-loss surfaces may be integral in designs for high-wind areas. Funneling of and orienting to prevailing breezes are desirable in warmer regions.

Altitude variation is an important facet of solar position and intensity. The sun changes altitude by about 47° from summer to winter solstice.

Solar orientation is basic to passive design, but exact orientation is not critical. While an orientation perpendicular to the sun's rays is optimum for heating, and although a tracking collector will maximize the capture of incoming energy, it is sometimes necessary to orient the building parallel to the sun's rays to minimize sun exposure.

The amount of sunlight and the clarity of the atmosphere vary the character of the microclimate. The quality of sun acting on a site will affect psychologically each person's physical comfort. A bright, sunny day in the tropics is not necessarily desirable, especially after a few hundred days without rain.

The tropical region that straddles the Equator has extensive exposure to direct sun rays. This can be an asset if properly utilized in providing solar energy. Otherwise, it can cause significant discomfort during the long summer days.

Passive Solar Application

The goal of passive solar application is to create structures that respond to the patterns of nature. The three basic principles are as follows:

- It must be designed to accept or reject solar heat when called for.
- It must have the thermal integrity to maintain internal comfort despite the range of climate forces acting on its weather skin.
- It must incorporate the ability to retain the presence or absence of heat within the building.

In some areas, comfort can be achieved through the use of an umbrella; in other areas, more complex arrangements may be necessary. These may be features in a building that are permanent, such as (1) insulation in walls and roofs to reduce heat flow, (2) overhang for shading walls, (3) selection of building materials with acceptable thermal qualities, (4) site orientation to reduce the effect of the sun on the building, and (5) the location of openings and the selection of materials for them, or active measures including (1) lighting controls, (2) operable shading devices such as screens and louvers, (3) a thermostat, or (4) the use of energy-efficient equipment.

PART THREE

Design Guidelines

CHAPTER 8

Application of Design Concepts

SITE SELECTION AND ANALYSIS

The appropriate design response to climate requires not only an intimate knowledge of the climatic conditions prevalent in the region but also the right "tools" to do the job. These include knowledge of the various design techniques to achieve the desired comfort level. Everything starts with the site. The right site for the project should be selected. Once the site is chosen, it should be analyzed and development strategies identified to respond to the information obtained.

The analysis should include the documentation and evaluation of the following data:

Site features: General condition of the site, landscape characteristics, topographic features, slope, vegetation, land type, soil condition.

Climate: Temperature, precipitation, humidity, wind direction, sunlight, sun paths, and sun angles as they relate to solar gain.

Other factors: Zoning classification, code restrictions and impact on site, utilities, access, slope, desirable/undesirable views, noise source/direction, local community, future neighbors, sewage treatment, water table, flood plains, the neighborhoods architectural "style," security

THE DESIGN PROCESS

The design process involves arranging the desired spaces within an envelope in close proximity to or remote from other related or unrelated spaces, with consideration given to circulation, views, wind, solar gain, and so on (see the bubble diagrams). The American Institute of Architects (AIA) Agreement between Owner and Architect divides the design sequence into five phases:

Bubble diagram—ground floor.

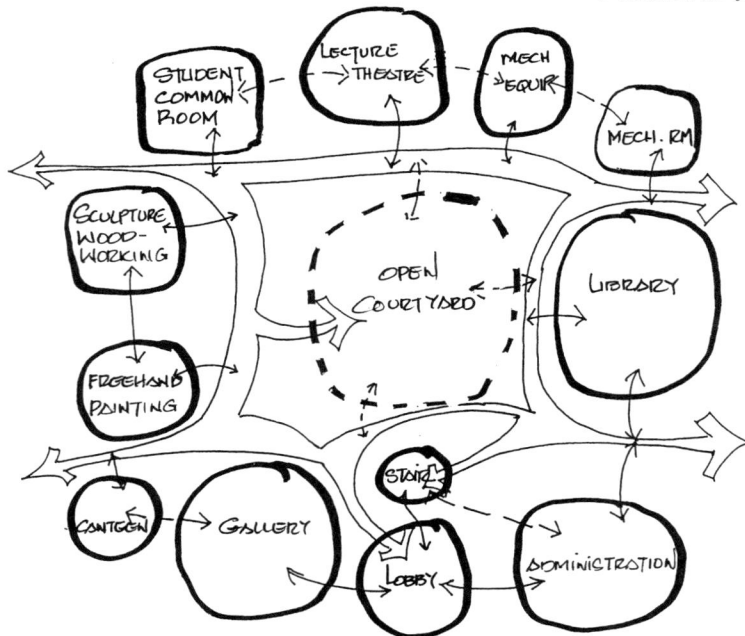

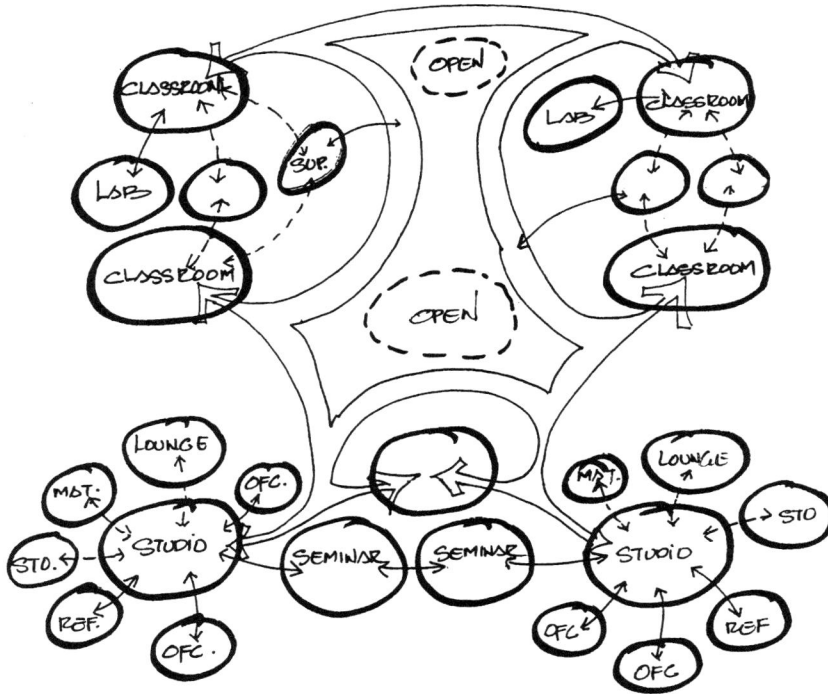

Bubble diagram—first floor.

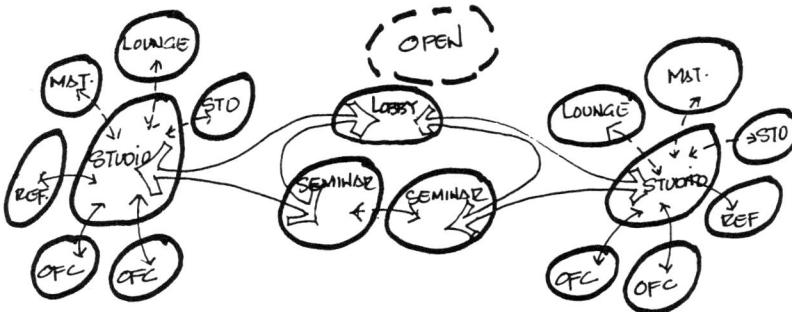

Bubble diagram—second floor.

Schematic design

Design development

Construction document

Bidding or negotiations

Construction administration

These phases can be adapted to the complexity and size of the project and the number of submittals required by the client. The end of each phase provides an ideal opportunity for progress reporting and client interface, and allows the architect to monitor and control the project.

DEVELOPING THE PLAN

The plan should work well with the site influences, the building's function, and the occupant's lifestyle (see figures). While developing the plan, the designer should:

Investigate a passive solar system that best suits the microclimate and the floor plan.

Size and locate windows, doors, skylights, solar chimneys, and so on best suited to the plan and site location. Consider courtyards, solar chimneys, and other features.

Sun and wind analysis: best orientation for sunshine.

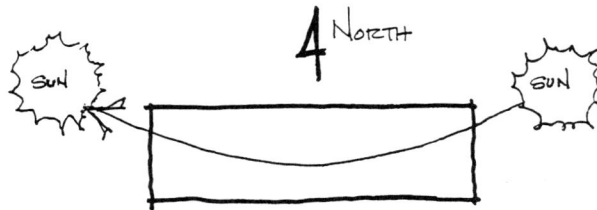

Sun and wind analysis: best orientation for wind.

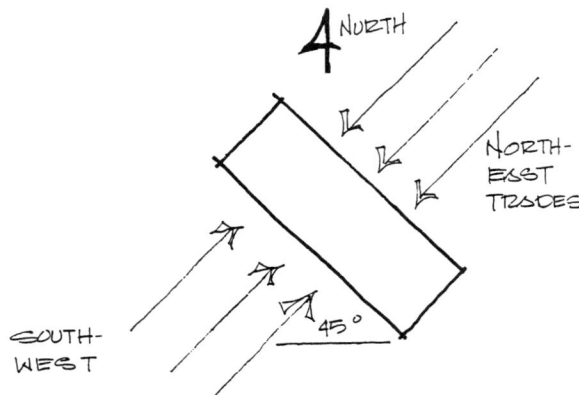

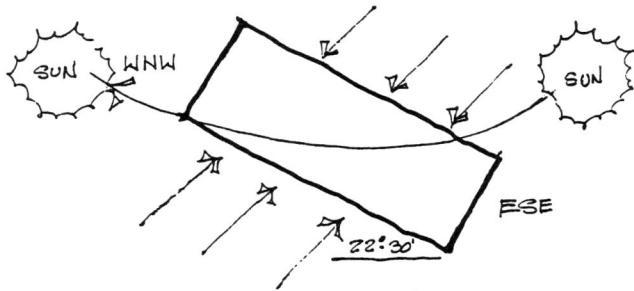

Sun and wind analysis: compromise orientation.

Select and develop exterior materials that not only work well with the external environment, but also have the thermal and insulation properties for the exterior surfaces. Rooms and zones should be sized to minimize unwanted infiltration of heat and loss of cold.

Examine the structure and determine the best marriage of the plan, solar system, structure, walls, foundation, openings, and so on.

Passive Solar Design: Basic Considerations

Building codes for energy conservation and the use of energy-efficient components in building design are becoming increasingly stringent. In addition, lending institutions (and utility companies) are recognizing the economic value of energy-conserving designs, which reduce operating costs by lowering energy consumption, thereby lowering their investment risk.

Energy-efficient techniques, when combined with conventional methods, have proven successful in reducing the demand for energy in buildings. Most of the techniques utilized in residential design are based on the use of solar radiation to heat water and to provide heat in colder climates. Solar energy for space cooling is also still occasionally used. The techniques can be divided into two categories: active and passive. In general, an active system employs roof-mounted solar panels, which require pumps and fans that depend on electricity as the power source. A passive system cools or heats without consuming electric power or any other nonrenewable source of energy.

There are three basic approaches to modern passive design:

Direct gain: This system utilizes south wall or clearstory windows as a means of gaining heat. It requires shading and overhangs during the long summer months.

Indirect gain: This approach incorporates a thermal storage wall, thermal storage roof, solar greenhouse, and natural convection loop.

Isolated gain: This system involves is a major separation between thermal storage and conditioned space.

The method chosen may need to be supplemented by appropriately located shading devices, as well as by adding moisture to or removing it from the ambient air to achieve the proper humidity/temperature levels.

This section is not intended to cover all aspects of solar design. Students and practitioners are encouraged to keep abreast of recent developments in this area. Instead, it addresses some of the elements of passive cooling in buildings designed for tropical climates.

Passive Solar System

The return to traditional design has resulted in increased interest in the passive solar system. The goal of this system is to achieve cooling and sometimes heating by relying primarily on the building's design rather than on mechanical means. In fact, the most efficient passive solar design is one that does not rely on the use of solar energy alone. In some climates, comfort can be attained with the aid of an electric fan. Although the introduction of a fan into the system makes it less than passive, it can be very effective in most homes. A passive solar system is successful if it reduces energy consumption when combined with a standard energy source. The system can be severely compromised, however, if the building is not properly designed. Some considerations for conserving energy consumption in buildings are as follows:

- Orient the building to maximize the effect of the trade winds.
- Use landscape for shading and wind channeling and, in some cases, to block out unwanted winds.
- Utilize overhangs to shade the building from excessive sunshine.
- Reduce windows and other openings on the south side of the building.

In the tropics, the living spaces in a well-designed passive-system home should face north. South-facing spaces and surfaces should be well shaded to prevent excessive solar heat gain. Shading elements should be sized to maximize the system's performance. If they are not properly sized, they could cause overheating during the long tropical summer months or block the natural light and the view. In addition to being blessed with an abundance of sunlight, the tropical environment is one of the most beautiful on earth. A well-designed tropical building should not only take advantage of the climate but should be designed to encourage interaction with the environment without compromising one's privacy.

Clearstories

Clearstories allow natural light to enter interior spaces but avoid the problems of privacy and glare. Clearstories can be vertical or tilted. They can become a nuisance if not properly installed, especially in the tilted position. If glass is chosen, special glazing may be necessary to prevent breakage.

Skylights

Skylights can be located flat or tilted on south-facing sloped roofs; horizontal positioning is more effective in allowing natural light to enter. One major disadvantage is that the sun's effect is maximum in the middle of summer, when the sun is highest in the sky, and minimum in the winter months, when the sun is lowest in the sky. Shading devices should be utilized when direct solar heat must be avoided and to reduce solar heat gain.

Storage

Solar energy can be stored in floors, walls, and ceilings of the interior spaces if these components have sufficient capacity to absorb and store cool air and to reradiate it or vent it back to the living space. The most common high-mass materials are concrete, brick, stone, and water. The amount of storage material needed will depend on the requirements of each installation. The material in a remote storage system is typically a rock bed usually located under the floor of the interior living space. Cool air is delivered to this bed when cool nighttime air is vented from the exterior through the full length of the material. The cool air is then delivered via ductwork to the outer spaces or used to flush the built-up daytime heat from the interior.

The following rules of thumb should be followed when designing a storage system (*The Passive Solar Construction Handbook,* Winters, Steven Associates, Inc. Copyright 1983, John Wiley & Sons, Inc.):

- The bed area should be 50 to 75 percent of the floor area of the living space.
- The bed should contain ½ to 3 cubic feet of fist-sized (2- to 3-inch-diameter) rocks per square foot of living area.
- The storage material should be loosely laid so that air voids exist between each unit.

- The material should be evenly distributed throughout the storage mass to ensure a balanced storage area.
- Storage materials should be located in an interior space away from direct sunlight.
- A storage mass placed horizontally will perform better than one in a vertical configuration.

Attached Sunspace

Attached sunspace, if properly designed, can be used for cooling in much the same manner as a verandah or porch, with the added advantage of heating to the adjacent space if needed. During warm to hot months exterior rooms can easily overheat, adding to the cooling load on the mechanical system. Therefore, the exterior collector surfaces should be well shaded to prevent unwanted heat gain. Deciduous trees and other types of vegetation can be used to provide shade, as well as other parts of the building such as projecting rooms, vertical or horizontal screens, louvers, shades, and overhangs. Sunspaces or exterior rooms should be properly vented. Where possible, low vents, to admit cool air, should be located in the shade on the windward side of the sunspace and high vents, to exhaust hot air, on the leeward side. Vents can be either operable or fixed. Gable vents on the east and west end walls are also recommended.

A storage mass located within the sunspace can also help keep the building cool. Locating vents adjacent to the storage mass will allow cool night air to pass over the mass and cool it. When properly shaded from the sun, this cooler mass will absorb heat generated in the sunspace during the day, thus cooling the space and ultimately the adjacent living areas. The collected heat will then be dissipated to the night air, completing the diurnal cycle. The cooling effect will be greatly enhanced by placing openings between the sunspace and the adjacent living spaces.

In additional to providing a buffer zone, sunspace can be used to grow houseplant and vegetables. It also extends the living space out, providing a shaded area for napping, lounging, and so on. As previously mentioned, shading is an integral part of passive systems and should be given serious consideration during the design phase.

Shading

Heat gain during the day can be avoided by providing a method for shading. The most effective shading devices are those placed on the exterior of the building, such as simple overhangs (fixed or adjustable), trellises, vegetation (deciduous trees, etc.), awnings, louvers (horizontal or vertical, fixed or adjustable), and wing walls.

Interior shading devices are generally easier to control but less effective than exterior units. Common interior shading devices include roller shades, blinds, drapes, and movable panels. These perform better if utilized during the day to block or limit the heat generated by direct sunlight.

Overhangs and Trellises

Although it is not cost effective to construct a south-facing overhang with a projection exceeding 2 feet, such overhangs are sometimes necessary to block the low evening sun and can be built using standard truss construction. Overhangs can also reduce potential glare in the warmer climates. They are popular and inexpensive if used within reasonable limits. A trellis system, another popular shading option for the tropics, is relatively inexpensive to build. Care should be taken to size each device properly to reduce the amount of sun reaching the exterior walls while allowing adequate light to enter the building. Trellises can be designed as simple extensions of the roofline and typically do not require maintenance. (See the section "Shade and Shading Devices" in Chapter 9.) The cooling effect can be greatly enhanced by allowing air to move across the exterior glass or wall surfaces.

In the cooler months the sun can be an asset in heating, but in the long summer months in almost all tropical climates it is necessary to keep it out. This is not particularly difficult, as the sun is low in the winter months and directly overhead in the summer. Shading for east and west façades is more difficult. Recommendations include minimizing the extent of east-west glazing and/or providing exterior control devices to limit exposure to direct sunlight and to prevent the trapping of heat. Because of the variation in the sun's position in the sky, it is impossible to provide shade in both spring and fall with fixed controls. The ideal control therefore is one that follows the sun or can be adjusted from within the building.

Lighting

The advent of artificial lighting has caused us to rely less on the sun for natural lighting. Thus, the windows are usually kept closed or opened only for views, and the lights are kept on all day. The downside of an artificial light source is that it adds heat to the interior space, providing a significant heat load for the cooling system. In temperate and warmer climates, the ideal application for exterior perimeter spaces is clear glass to take advantage of natural lighting when conditions permit, protected by exterior shading from the direct rays of the sun.

Energy Conservation and Comfort

The heat generated by lights, equipment, and people adds to the overall space heat that must be removed by the cooling system. Dramatic energy and cost savings can be achieved by simply altering the levels of interior temperature and ventilation. This can be done by raising the temperature in areas occupied only for short periods of time or by shutting down individual cooling units of unoccupied spaces such as conference rooms, meeting halls, and cafeterias. The entire air-conditioning system should be shut down at night and during the days when the building is unoccupied. If this is impractical because of the time needed to reestablish the desired temperature, controls can be installed to activate the equipment a few hours before the building is used instead of operating the system all night or throughout the weekend.

Most of the energy in an air-conditioning system is used to lower the temperature and relative humidity of the air to achieve the desired comfort level. Increasing the temperature and humidity setting by 2°, especially for spaces that are seldom used, significantly reduces the energy demands on the mechanical system. Once optimal temperature and humidity are attained, the system uses a large percentage of recycled air to maintain these levels during the day. Flushing the building's interior with cool night air before restarting the system, and increasing the temperature and humidity settings, result in great energy savings without serious discomfort to users.

BUILDING CODES: MINIMUM SAFETY REQUIREMENTS

Public concern for safety in building construction in the developed world has resulted in the formulation of rules and regulations called *building codes*. The earliest building laws were concerned with collapse. During the reigns of Julius Caesar and Augustus Caesar a speculative high-rise apartment building collapsed, prompting the Romans to restrict the height of buildings. These were limited to 70 feet (21 m) and, later, when 70 feet was found unsatisfactory, to 60 feet (18 m).

The Romans required the contractors who built their stone bridges to put up a deposit to ensure that the bridge would not collapse. If the bridge was still in good shape forty years later, the deposit was returned to the client. Later, notably in London in the 14th century, regulations were introduced to prevent fire and restrict its spread. On the other hand, the general lack of building codes or regulations in the past, although extremely costly in lives and structures, allowed architects and builders to experiment with new designs and materials.

Current building codes are the result of years of experience with the experiments of the past (some costly). They have been compiled by knowledgeable engineers, politicians, and architects to regulate the design and construction of buildings and the quality of building materials. Although most of the codes in use today do not protect against storm surges, local building officials in storm hazard areas often adopt national codes that contain building requirements for protection against high wind and water.

It is worth emphasizing that the purpose of these codes is to provide minimum standards to safeguard lives, health, and property. These codes protect persons from themselves as well as from their neighbors.

A building code is not a guarantee of safety; the code is only as good as its enforcement. Beach communities, for example, often develop so rapidly that it is often difficult for even well-qualified building inspectors to keep up with code inspections. Code development is often compressed into the off-season or during posthurricane reconstruction and is economically driven, which results in codes being too lightly enforced or enforced by individuals unqualified to be building inspectors.

A code should contain the basic principles and guidelines to be followed to achieve safety and yet permit creative thinking and innovation on the part of the designer. On the other hand, the code must provide sufficient details to guide the nontechnical builder (small contractors, home owners) to develop a safe structure, yet give leeway for the creative architect and engineer.

CHAPTER 9

Design and Construction Techniques

SITE PLANNING

Radiation reflected from the ground into the building can add to the cooling requirements of the structure, as the solar radiation received by the ground surface in summer is about twice that received by either the east or west walls. The solar heat load can be minimized by selecting exterior surface material of low reflectivity. Reflection from outdoor surfaces cannot be controlled as easily as direct radiation because it is diffused or nondirectional. The radiation reflected onto a vertical wall will be one-half the amount reflected from the horizontal surface. The greatest concern, therefore, is the area immediately outside the building. Although locating an asphalt driveway outside a wall will keep reflected radiation at a minimum, the heat absorbed by the paving will make the air temperature outside the wall much higher than that over the lawn and most other surfaces. Sun and ground cover make effective sun absorbers and cool the air by evaporation.

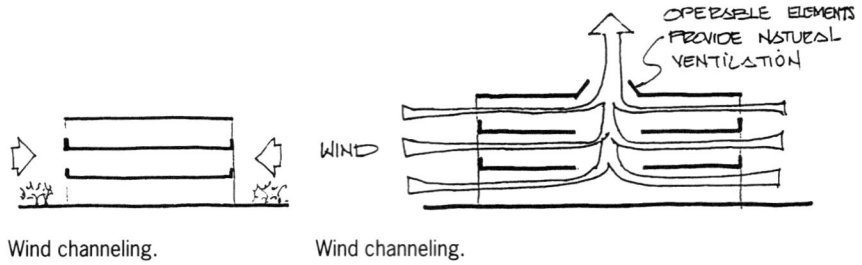

Wind channeling.

Wind channeling.

Ventilation

Adequate ventilation must be provided in buildings for a number of reasons. Air movement replaces stuffy used air, illuminates smoke and odor, and evacuates unwanted warm air. Although ventilation can be used effectively for cooling, it is also needed for heating. Most passive solar heating systems utilize a radiant thermal mass; some air motion and exchange can occur without adversely affecting the heating process. To allow passive ventilation to take place, vents have to be properly sized and located to allow every space within a building to adapt to various seasonal demands.

The direction and speed of air flow determine the cooling effect of natural ventilation. The dry-bulb, still-air temperature is effectively lowered 5°F if the air is moved at a velocity of 6 miles per minute. Air speed can adjusted for comfort by opening and closing a variety of properly placed windows. To promote ventilation, there must be an inlet and an outlet on opposite or adjacent sides of a space or building. Air flow into an opening on the windward side of a space is most effective when the wind direction is within 30° of normal to the opening. Wind scoops, vegetation, and the type of window can be used to channel air into openings from any direction. On the downward side, openings should be larger than on the windward side. This creates a maximum suction effect, facilitating free air movement through a space.

Courtyards increase natural ventilation.

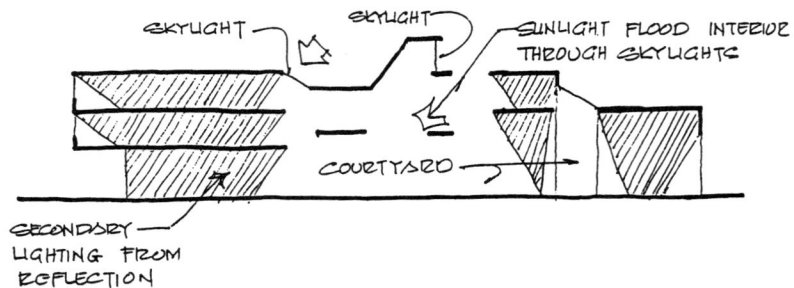

Locating Openings

Doors and windows are the natural means of ventilating houses. The placement, size, and type of openings govern the effectiveness of the elevation. Some building codes require all habitable rooms of dwellings to have an operable exterior opening measuring not less than 1/29th of the floor area, with a minimum of 5 square feet.

Windows can be oriented to catch or slow down prevailing breezes. Awning windows allows air to enter but keep rain out. Basement windows can open to catch or buffer wind. Louvered openings permit uninhibited air flow. Hopper windows allow free upward motion. Since warm air rises and expands, outside air should be brought in low and exited high for ideal cooling.

Operable skylights make effective ventilators and allow natural illumination. Good commercial units permit opening to the degree desired and seal well when closed, keeping moisture out and minimizing infiltration. Always use double-glazed types for increased insulation. Pressure-spring skylights open upward, and restraining chains are used to adjust the opening and for closing. Crank-type skylights are generally superior. Operable skylights have the advantage of always being exposed to the wind, regardless of where it comes from. In areas of driving rains or heavy winds, it is wise to orient the opening away from the direction of the storm. Operable skylights are good choices for ventilating bathrooms and kitchens.

Solar Chimneys

Solar chimneys, plenums, or black boxes, located where the sun can warm them, use solar heat to reinforce natural air convection. As a black metal chimney gets hot during the day, the air inside heats, expands, and rises, pulling interior air up and out. One advantage of the solar chimney is its ability to self-balance; the hotter the day, the hotter the chimney and the faster the air movement.

A solar air ramp, windows with radiant barrier curtains, or a solar mass wall can be used for induction vents. Where sunlight is trapped behind south or west glazing, air is heated and rises. If the heated air is allowed to vent outside at the top, interior air will be sucked up the solar-heated space and exhausted. This exiting air should be replaced by outside air taken from a low, shaded spot, preferably on the north or east side.

Courtyards

Many cultures have utilized the interior courtyard for cooling. This open, shaded space can be covered by lightweight shading lattice

Operable elements provide natural ventilation.

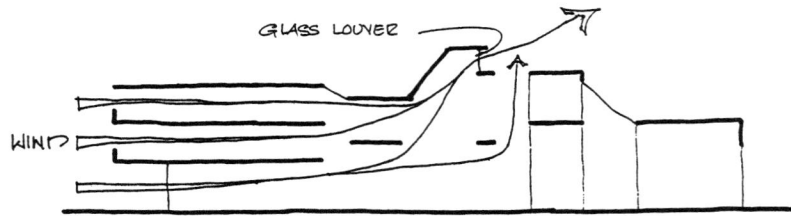

during the heat of the day to prevent sun intrusion and heat buildup in the interior walls. Vegetation and fountains or ponds add evaporation to the cooling effect of the breezes passing in one side of the building and out the other. At night, by opening all doors and windows and removing the day shade, deep-space radiation, air, and evaporative cooling continually remove heat from the walls.

BUILDING FORM AND ORIENTATION

The amount of solar heat received by the surface of a house can be minimized for any period of the year through manipulation of the (1) shape and orientation of the building plan with respect to the sun; (2) height of the building exposed to the sun; and (3) shape and pitch of the roof. Solar gain can be minimized by orienting the façade to face due north and south.

Patios, porches, courtyards, and other protected outdoor living areas can contribute to the comfort of the indoors, as well as providing pleasant private living spaces. In summer, porches and patio covers, for example, shade the house walls, openings, surroundings, and outdoor floor surfaces. This helps to keep the temperature of the outdoor air low, making natural ventilation more suitable and minimizing conductive heat gain through walls.

Since summer irradiation is always most intense on a horizontal surface, it is useful to decrease roof areas and increase building heights; walls are more easily shaded than roofs. In general, for solar control, a building in the southern regions of Jamaica should be taller than a building in the northern regions that encloses the same interior volume.

In cooler areas of mountainous regions, where controlled solar heat gain becomes necessary, the general concept of using south-facing room planning can be carried one step further by creating an interior room such as a sun room or atrium with a maximum ability to function as a direct-gain solar system. This room may be ideal as a recreation area, sitting room, or working greenhouse. Heat gained from the sun room can be removed from this room by natural convention or by a temperature-controlled fan for distribution throughout the rest of the house or for thermal storage.

Planning specific rooms or functions to coincide with solar orientation is still the most energy-efficient technique available. A house can be made more energy efficient if it is designed so that the order of rooms in which the normal daily sequence of activities occurs follows the path of the sun. This strategy is complemented by and most effective when the interior is partitioned into separate heating and cooling zones. By relating zones to sun movement, solar energy can be put to use when it is most available by direct orientation, and mechanical heating or cooling can be minimized.

Approximately 20 percent of the energy consumed is used to heat and cool buildings. However, in spite of dwindling energy resources worldwide, many buildings today are still designed without regard to the sun's impact on and potential contribution to space heating and cooling. When deciding on the rough shape of a building, it is necessary to think about limiting the sunlight that enters the building and admitting only the amount needed to collect solar radiation.

A building elongated along the east-west axis will expose more surface area to the south during the winter for the collection of solar radiation while minimizing eastern and western exposure to the direct morning and evening sun. This is also the most efficient shape, in all climates, for minimizing cooling requirements in the summer and heating requirements in the winter. The optimum shape of a building is one that loses a minimum amount of heat in the winter and gains a minimum amount of heat in the summer.

For any given building volume, the more compact the shape, the less heat it loses. The surface-to-volume (SVR) ratio is a measure of the efficiency of enclosing space, but it does not express how efficiently the enclosed space is used for living. The benefit of different building configurations can be determined by comparing the SVR of alternative plans that contain the same interior volume space. The designer should endeavor to minimize the outside wall and roof areas (ratio of exterior surface to enclosed volume) to reduce the heat gain on a building.

Shade and Shading Devices

The impact of solar radiation on buildings in hot climates must be reduced, not only by orientation and effective design of the structure but also by adequate shading. Although it is not always convenient or economical to shade roofs, walls lend themselves to this treatment in a number of ways that can be invaluable for eliminating or reducing one of the greatest sources of heat gain: solar radiation entering through

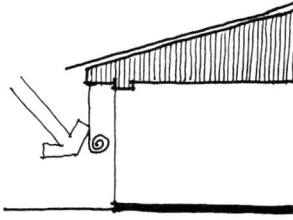

Exterior shades.

windows. Various methods are available for screening walls and windows. When deciding on the shading requirements, each façade must be considered separately to achieve the most effective solar control. Shading devices not only reflect heat onto a building but also trap hot air, as well as conducting heat inward through the structure.

Comfort can be maintained in tropical regions through passive measures. Where cooling is desired at various times of the day, in different seasons, or even throughout the year, the appropriate method must be considered. Hot-dry, hot-humid, windy-dry, windy-humid, and other prevailing conditions dictate the approach to be used. Often shading, cooling, and ventilation should be integrated to allow for seasonal or daily variations.

Shading the exterior, interior, and surrounding areas of a structure is the first line of action to reduce the temperature buildup due to ambient air or solar incidence. By limiting the amount of heat buildup in the thermal mass of a building, cooling requirements are reduced. A structure that is properly designed for its climate will

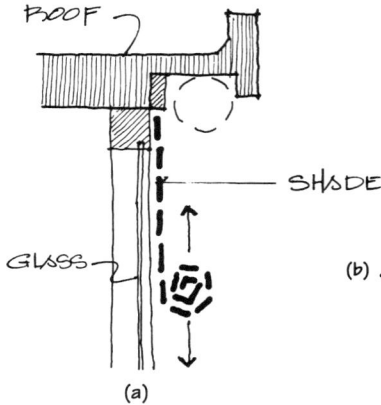

(a) Exterior shades.
(b) Covered ways within buildings.
(c) Covered ways through buildings.
(d) Covered ways between buildings.

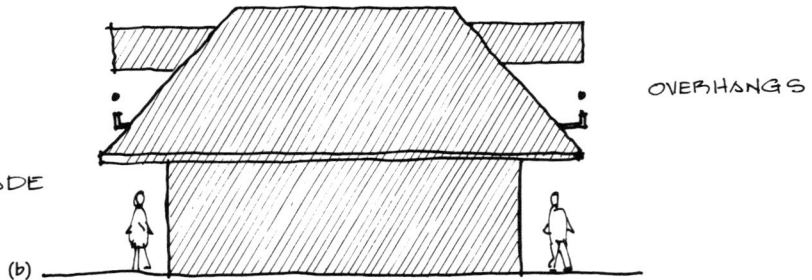

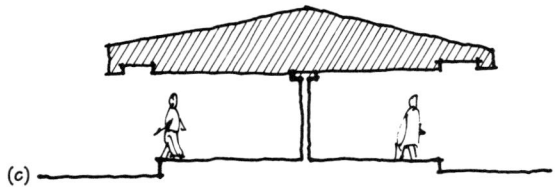

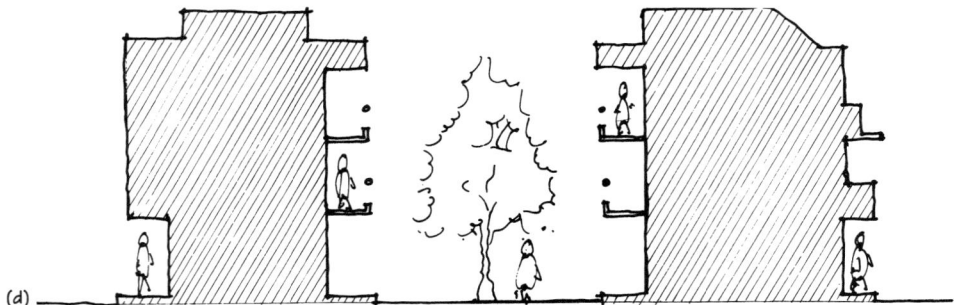

need little, if any, conventional equipment to achieve comfort for most users.

The planting of trees, bushes, or vines in appropriate places can shade structures adequately in tropical climates. When attempting to cut solar gain into a building, it is important to interrupt the sun's energy before it strikes the glass or walls. Once the heat has penetrated the envelope of a structure, it must be removed from the interior, which may require additional unnecessary steps.

Evergreen trees planted to the north of the building act as buffers, helping to block winds and storms. Further, they can act as evaporative coolers, lowering the temperature of air passing through the branches and needles. They also shade the ground around buildings, preventing heat buildup in the earth and thus modifying the microclimate. Glades and oases illustrate this effect in hot climates.

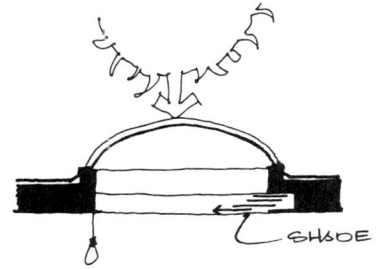

Interior shades.

Vegetation

Trees and shrubs provide the simplest way of protecting a low building (or part of it) from solar radiation. Deciduous trees are especially valuable, as they do not block winter sunshine.

The beneficial effect of plant cover is considerable and should be taken into account by the designer. However, although vegetation provides protection from glare, dust, and erosion, it also has disadvantages when planted too close to the building. Roots can damage foundations and drain pipes, leaves can block gutters, and desirable air movement can be reduced or diverted away over the building.

In heavily planted areas in both summer and winter, average temperature drops by only a few degrees. In the daytime, the top of a forest is heated by solar radiation. The remaining cool air, being heavier than the warmer air, will sinks to ground level.

Ground Planting

Row shrubs, bushes, and grasses can be planted around buildings where a view is desired. They reduce reflection of solar energy from

TALL CANOPY TREES ON SOUTH SIDE OF HOUSE WILL SHADE ROOF AND WALL

Vegetation for sun shading. (Watson, D.: *Climatic Design* (1983), Reproduced with permission of the McGraw-Hill Companies)

roadways, walks, patios, sand, and bodies of water. These plantings, when watered in the morning, will cool passing air, evaporatively cooling the area around the structure and reducing secondary heating effects.

Deciduous trees, such as fruit and ornamental trees, are particularly suitable for planting on the south, east, and west sides or in courtyards of buildings. Their spring, fall, and summer foliage interrupts the flow of solar energy before it strikes the ground, window, or wall surfaces. These species defoliate in the late fall, and the loss of leaves allows solar heat to warm collection surfaces where applicable, as well as evaporate surface water.

Vines and climbers can be planted to shade east, west, and south façades. Plant boxes on roofs and walls create hanging screens of foliage, shading windows and walls. A lattice or trellis will accommodate climbing plants to form a similar screen, blocking the sun yet allowing cooling breezes to flow through.

Roof Planting

Sod roofs or rooftop vines are valuable in many climates. A properly constructed roof, when covered with earth and planted, may never wear out. The earth prevents the injurious effects of sunlight, wind, and wet-dry cycles on the roof's moisture membrane.

In dry climates, irrigation of roof plants will do much to cool a structure through evaporation. A moist roof will lose the heat absorbed during the day to the night sky. Roof planting should be well irrigated to prevent the shallow roots from drying out and preventing fire.

GLARE

One of the problems in hot climates is excluding not only radiant heat but also glare, while at the same time admitting sufficient daylight. In this situation, as in many others, there is a fundamental difference between arid and humid regions.

In arid areas, glare arises mainly when sunlight is reflected from the surface of the ground and from light-colored walls of other buildings. A traditional way of overcoming this problem is to keep windows on the external elevations small and few in number, with the larger, low-level windows overlooking the shaded interior courtyard. When small windows are used on external walls, care must be taken in their design and location to ensure that glare is not exaggerated by too sharp a contrast between the bright opening and the surrounding inside wall surface. Traditional solutions to this problem are vertical slit windows—usually in the corners of the rooms—windows placed between the ceiling and eye level, and various forms of lattices, screens, or shutters to filter external brightness.

High humidity and typically overcast conditions in the warm-wet regions result in a high proportion of solar radiation being diffused. In this case, the sky is the main source of glare, which can become almost unbearable. Because it is usual to have large openings for cross-ventilation, low overhanging eaves or wide verandahs are used to obstruct the view of most of the sky. In traditional houses, thin external walls of coarsely woven mats, which can sometimes be rolled up, maximize the effect of every breeze and admit good-quality light while completely eliminating glare and providing privacy.

Settlers in the hot areas of Southern California, Jamaica, and Australia built a wide verandah surrounding their houses, which provided sitting and sleeping space in an intermediate zone (between indoors and outdoors) even in rainy weather. These verandahs also shaded the walls and windows and offered protection from glare, as well as allowing continuing ventilation during violent storms. This sensible solution had certain disadvantages, however; interiors tended to be rather gloomy, and the sun was eliminated from the interior even during the underheated period of the year. One solution to this problem is to use a pergola-covered verandah over which creepers, which lose their leaves in winter, are grown.

DAY LIGHTING

Sunlight in the tropics is intense despite the cloudy skies. Clouds dampen the effect of sunlight, making it more bearable than the arid deserts. They act as a roof, absorbing sunlight, and overhang the earth with watery pressure. This is then radiated to the earth in its brilliance. In tropical house design, the tendency is to increase window and door openings, shade the heat, and block the glare from any part of the sky above and reflected from ground surfaces nearby. A building should be well shaded from sun and glare, with light filtering through vegetation or screens, and with the ability to admit and control abundant air for ventilation.

HORIZONTAL SCREENS

Horizontal screens are most effective against high sun and are normally used on the north or south sides of buildings. The nearer one is to the Equator, the easier it is to screen façades with a roof overhang such as those most often used in warm-wet regions. The overhang is generally sufficient to protect the interior of the dwelling from slanting sun and driving rain, as well as to shade part of the surrounding area throughout the day. Balconies and projecting floor slabs are also common forms of horizontal screening.

Overhangs should exclude sun during summer and, if necessary, admit it in winter. Shading of both the north and south walls must be considered if a building is situated in the tropics.

VERTICAL SCREENS

Vertical screens in the form of closely spaced columns, vertical fins, or rotating louvers are useful against the low sun on the east and west façades. Combined vertical and horizontal screening—the egg-crate grill, for example—can be effective for buildings with any orientation, depending on its depth and the dimensions of the openings. Whatever type of screening is used, it should be placed outside the glazing; should be constructed of low-thermal-capacity materials to ensure quick cooling after sunset; and should be designed to prevent not only reflection on any part of the building but also the trapping of hot air.

Solar charts devised for several countries and a shadow angle protractor can be used to calculate shadow requirements and check the efficiency of the proposed screening for any orientation, any time of the day, and any day of the year. The use of these charts is described in detail in various books. A shading mask can also be produced using a shadow angle protractor. Any solid object placed between the sun and the center of the diagram (point of observation) will cast a shadow on this point. The situation can also be reversed with the same effect; the light source can be placed at the point of observation and the shadow cast on the sky vault. The areas of the sky vault covered by the shadow are the portions of the sky from which no light can reach the point of observation as long as the solid or opaque object is present. If the sun itself moves through such an area of the sky vault, clearly the point of observation will then be in shade and receive no direct light from the sun.

Any object composed of regular geometric lines has a characteristic shading mask, which represents the section of the sky that it will obscure. In many cases, different shading devices leave similar masks, so several possible solutions to a shading problem exist. The designer, in other words, may decide early in the process what shading performance (or mask) is needed while retaining the freedom to select an appropriate device. In his book *Design with Climate,* Olgyay has suggested the following four steps for designing and examining shading devices:

1. Determine the times when shading is needed (the overheated period).
2. Determine the position of the sun during the period when shading is needed using a sun path diagram.
3. Determine the type and position of the shading device for the overheated period. The position of the device is plotted on a protractor that has the same scale as the sun path diagram. Shading masks are independent of latitude, orientation, and time and can be used in any situation. Most shading devices produce shading masks that can be easily resolved into one of the three basic types: vertical, where the characteristic shape is bounded by radial lines; horizontal, with a mask of segmental shape; and egg crate, which is a combination of the first two.
4. Evaluate the shading device and determine its dimensions to ensure correct shading during the overheated period and to allow, if necessary, some sun to penetrate during the under-heated period.

Steps 3 and 4 can be reversed; the required shading can be determined and an appropriate shading device then developed.

HURRICANES

Hurricanes are a natural and expected part of the dynamic equilibrium of the tropics and are broadly classified as tropical storms. The terms *hurricane* and *typhoon* are regionally specific names for a strong tropical cyclone. *Tropical cyclone* is the term for a nonfrontal, synoptic-scale, low-pressure system over tropical or subtropical waters with organized convection (i.e., thunderstorm activity) and defined cyclonic surface wind circulation.

If winds reach 33 m/s (64 kt), the storm is called a *hurricane* (the north Atlantic Ocean, the northeast Pacific Ocean east of the international date line, or the South Pacific Ocean east of 160E); a *typhoon* (the northwest Pacific Ocean west of the international date line); a *severe tropical cyclone* (the southwest Pacific Ocean west of 160E or the southeast Indian Ocean east of 90E); a *severe cyclonic storm* (the north Indian Ocean); or a *tropical cyclone* (the southwest Indian Ocean) (Neuman, 1993).

Note that the definition of *maximum sustained surface winds* depends upon who is taking the measurements. The World Meteorology Organization's guidelines suggest utilizing a ten-minute average to get a sustained measurement. Most countries utilize this as the standard. However, the National Hurricane Center and the Joint Typhoon Warning Centers of the United States use a one-minute averaging period to get a sustained measurement. This difference may cause complications in comparing the statistics from one basin to another, as using a smaller averaging period may slightly raise the number of occurrences (Neuman, 1993).

Hurricanes are large, violent disturbances with winds rotating about a low-pressure center. They begin as low-pressure areas over tropical ocean regions. A hurricane evolves from a tropical disturbance through a tropical depression into a tropical storm, which then becomes a genuine hurricane. A *tropical disturbance* is a moving area of thunderstorms. A *tropical depression* is a low-pressure area with winds of up to 38 mph (61 kilometers per hour, km/h) and rotary circulation. A *tropical storm* has winds ranging from 39 to 73 mph (63 to 117 km/h) and counterclockwise circulation. A *hurricane* is a tropical storm whose winds equal or surpass 74 mph (119 km/h). In the center of the hurricane is the much-heralded eye, a region of calm and cloudlessness, 10 to 20 miles (16 to 32 km) in diameter. As the eye passes, the calm may last anywhere from a few minutes to an hour.

Hurricanes in the Northern Hemisphere always rotate to the left, or counterclockwise, responding to the rotation of the earth. Tropical storms begin when air currents begin to flow into a low-pressure area from a surrounding higher-pressure zone, much as air rushes into a vacuum. A trajectory along the surface of the earth in the Northern Hemisphere, be it an artillery shell, an ocean current, or a wind current, is deflected to the right. The force causing this deflection is the earth's rotation, and it is referred to as the *Coriollis force*. The net effect is a counterclockwise flowing circulation. Hurricanes gain energy from the evaporation of warm ocean water. They quickly lose energy when they reach land because the sea, their source of energy, no longer is available.

Hurricanes developing in the north Atlantic Ocean and off the Caribbean usually strike the eastern United States and the Gulf Coast, with devastating results. On the average, six hurricanes occur off the coast of the United States per year. Most occur in August, September, and October. The hurricane season is considered to be the six-month period from June 1 to December 1. Because of the extensive damage that can be caused not only by the direct effects of wind and excessive rainfall, but also by the secondary effects of flooding, storm surges, and landslides, these cyclonic storms are potentially one of the most damaging of all natural phenomena.

In areas where there is any chance of tropical storms occurring, it is essential for the designer to ascertain whether there are any codes in force (codes ranging from performance types to specification types are used in the United States, Japan, Jamaica, and the Bahamas), as well as to collect all available records of former storms. In addition to reliable meteorological data, case histories and newspaper reports can be very useful. For coastal areas that are subject to cyclonic storms and do not have codes, the United Nations has proposed a scale that provides some means of comparing the effects of storms of various intensities. In this regard, it should be noted that the destructive power of wind increases with the square of its speed, so that a tenfold increase in wind speed increases its force 100 times.

Effects of Wind

A high-rise building constructed near the shore will be subjected to both lateral wind pressure and increased upward pressure, so wind forces must be considered in building design. The U.S. Uniform Building Code specifies that at most inland locations a structure up to 30 feet (90 m) high (two or three stories) should withstand 15 pounds of wind pressure per square foot (718 Newtons per square meter, n/m^2), whereas the same structure on a shore with a hurricane history should withstand 40 pounds per square foot (1.9 kn/m^2). This 250 percent increase applies to higher buildings; for example, at 100 feet (30 m, ten stories) the design pressure needs to be 30 psf (1.4 kn/m^2) inland, as opposed to 75 psf (3.6 kn/m^2) on the shore. This means that if you are living inland in a two-story house and move to the eleventh floor of a high-rise on the shore, you should expect five times more wind pressure than you are accustomed to. This can be a great—and possibly devastating—surprise.

High wind pressure can create unpleasant motion of the building, to the point of causing motion sickness to occupants. Older skyscrapers with heavy masonry construction were not as susceptible to wind-induced sway because their considerable mass reduced the motion. In the last two decades, however, the density of tall buildings has dropped to about half of their earlier value, accompanied by a reduction in stiffness and damping. The increase in flexibility and sway and the decrease in damping are undesirable side effects of modern construction, permitting more windows to pop out, walls to crack, and discomfort to be felt by inhabitants.

Airborne debris from high winds is a major threat. The damage caused by hurricanes Allen and David prompted the Building Codes Department to enact new requirements for glazing and construction for hurricane-prone areas. A prospective resident can ask the builder or owner about the type of glass used. Certainly, such measures as shutters, smaller panes, and stronger glass can decrease wind damage. Inside drapes can lessen injury from shattered glass, especially that caused by small flying objects. The heavier the drapes, the better suited they are for this purpose.

Sitework: Buildings can be protected by planting trees not less than 50 feet (15 m) away. In coastal areas, where high tidal surges are likely, buildings should be constructed on earth mounds or raised on stilts (timber poles or concrete columns) so that the floor level of the structure is sufficiently elevated above the high water level.

Foundation: Should be broad so that it can transfer a portion of the force that arises to the ground.

Structure: Buildings raised on stilts are more liable to uplift, and particular care should be taken with their design. In all cases, extra-strong joints are required between foundations and walls, as well as between walls and floor slabs or roofs, by means of steel reinforcing, bolts, and so on. Heavy material should be utilized as much as possible, and sufficient diagonal bracing should be provided for stability.

Roofs: All roof elements, such as purlins and cladding materials, should be securely fixed. The use of canopies and overhangs should be minimized and, where possible, brackets that can be used to tie down the roof between storm seasons should be provided.

Windows: Windows and doors can be a particular source of danger if they are broken. Wind has easy access to the interior, and the resultant uplift pressure on the roof can destroy the entire building. Window frames should be securely anchored, and large glass areas should be protected by shutters.

SITE SELECTION IN HURRICANE AREAS

The least desirable area for buildings on an island is where the island is narrow or low or lacks much dune protection. Flat, straight roads that extend to the beach should be avoided. Allow for at least 100 feet (30 m) between the site and the first dune, and preferably 200 feet (60 m). Beware of unstable bluffs. The important decision is to ensure safety for both the structure and the lives of its inhabitants. One should consider what type of shoreline should be chosen: hard rock or unconsolidated cliffs, coastal plain mainland beaches, barrier island open-ocean beaches, lagoon or bay beaches, or rocky shores Pilkey, "Coastal Design" (1983). One consolation is that from a safety standpoint this may be a distinct advantage, as the least expensive lots in beach communities tend to be the least dangerous and the most expensive ones the most dangerous. Once the area has been chosen, the site search must be narrowed further. Evaluation of individual sites can be very complex, but the single most important factor is clearly elevation. The higher the better, provided, of course, that it is not high atop the edge of an eroding cliff. The final major decision is what type of structure should be built or bought.

SITE SELECTION ALONG A COASTLINE

Before choosing a site along any coastline, one should first look over any assessment and the *Atlas of Shoreline Erosion*. If a proposed homesite is described in this publication as having an erosion problem or being artificially protected, one should beware. If a sea view is imperative, choose higher ground and build on stable rock.

The higher the elevation, the better. Although few waves over 12 feet (4 m) have been spotted along the California coast, 40-foot (12-m) waves were measured near La Jolla in 1940. More recently (1998) El Niño caused great damage, eroding beachfront and hillside properties along the Pacific Coast Highway.

Solid rock with few joints and no layering is the ideal, but such rock types are not common along most shores. Walk the site and analyze the rock formation and soil condition. Avoid any bluff made up of lightly cemented material that can be scraped away with a shovel or hand pick.

Consult with local or state offices for maps showing land-slip hazard areas. Walk the beach, consult with residents, and review public records for a history of bluff collapse. Take precautions if there is evidence of landslide material at the base of the cliff on the beach. Do not consult with realtors or developers on this matter.

Stay away from any prospective development that has been bulldozed to improve the view, if drainpipes have been installed on the bluff face, or if other things have been done that might increase the rate of bluff erosion. Again, walk on the beach and look for evidence of fresh erosion or bluff failure. Be very skeptical if you hear that there is no erosion, or that erosion can be stopped. Preventing or stopping erosion can be costly.

Are nearby rivers dammed upstream? If so, the sand supply from river to beach may be greatly reduced, which may lead to drastic reduction in the size of your beach and ultimately a perceived need for costly engineering measures. Groins, jetties, and sea walls on adjacent beaches may also result in a cutoff of sand supply to your beach, causing it to erode.

A potential tidal wave will determine the minimum safe elevation, depending on the homesite location. Local officials will have flood maps (if the community is eligible for the National Flood Insurance Program) that can tell you if you are at a dangerous elevation from the standpoint of storm flooding.

Landslides along coastlines may be caused by either a natural geologic deficiency or a manmade problem. Evidence of a previous landslide should raise a warning flag to a prospective buyer or builder.

An earthquake hazard area may also be associated with landsliding.

DESIGN OF BUILDINGS IN HURRICANE AREAS

Buildings must be designed to withstand hurricane forces in any direction. Hurricanes blow in a circular path around the storm center, and winds may blow first from one direction and then from the other as the storm moves forward. Well-designed, well-constructed buildings can withstand a wind force of up to 150 mph without damage except that caused by flying debris. A conventional structure is normally built to resist vertical downward loads (its own weight), plus live loads (contents, people, snow) on the floor and roof. When a storm hits, the forces can be upward (uplift), sideward, or from any direction. Both pressure and suction are applied. On the coast, all the components of a building need to be connected. Rafters to column, column to trusses, and truss rafters to walls must be securely fastened together with adequate anchors or clips. All structural members (beams, rafters, columns) should be held fast to each other on the assumption that about 25 percent of the vertical load on each member may be a force coming from either the transverse (sideways) or upward direction. Correct construction technique adds very little to the cost of the house.

Foundation

A proper foundation is critical for buildings built adjacent to a shoreline. This is especially true for high-rise buildings on barrier islands. Major storms or gradual erosion responding to the sea-level rise may

SPIRAL COLUMNS, 20" Φ.
ALL FOOTINGS 8'-0" SQ..
MAX. COL. LOAD
350,000 #

25'-0"   25'-0"

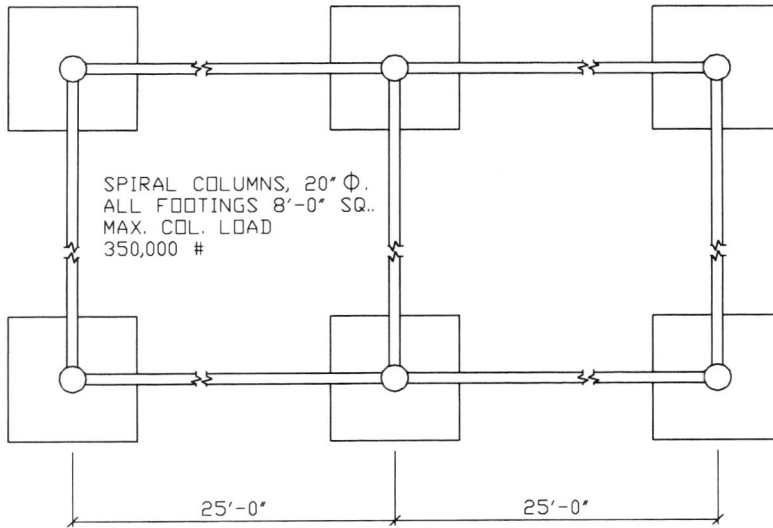

Separate footings connected with ties.

undercut buildings. Pilings are the first line of defense against such an occurrence. In theory, any large high-rise in a beach area should be capable of withstanding complete removal by waves of several feet of sand from beneath it and still stand firmly on deeply rooted pilings.

Resistance to lateral wind forces generally requires either rigidity or bracing; one solution to the problem commonly used by primitive builders is flexibility: the use of tied joints, which allows structures to sway and give in the winds, much like a palm tree. Another method is to avoid the problem altogether by sinking the building below ground level.

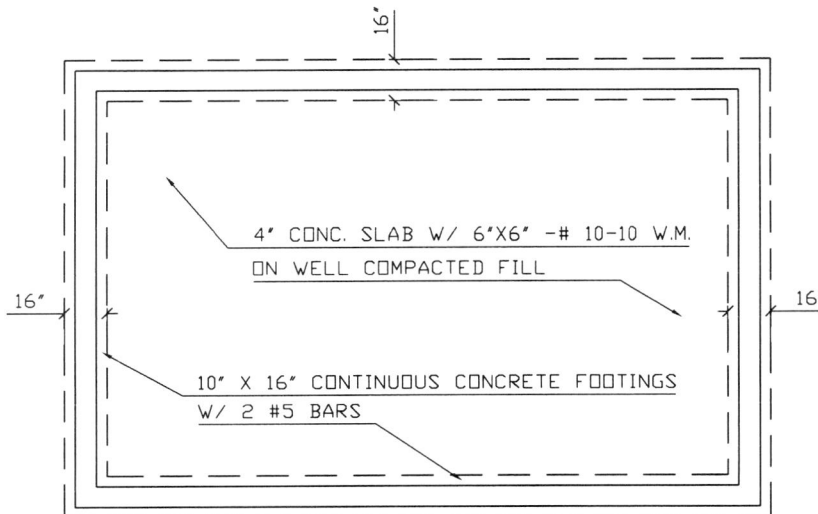

16'

4" CONC. SLAB W/ 6"X6" -# 10-10 W.M.
ON WELL COMPACTED FILL

16'   16'

10" X 16" CONTINUOUS CONCRETE FOOTINGS
W/ 2 #5 BARS

Foundation plan for a one-story house.

METAL COPING

REINF. CONC. PARAPET

REINF. CONC. BOND BEAM

EMBEDDED STL. ANCHOR

8" CONCRETE BLOCKWALL

CEMENT PLASTER

FINISH GRADE

GRAVEL ON BUILT-UP ROOF

LIGHTWEIGHT CONCRETE

OPEN WEB STEEL JOIST

PLASTER CEILING

PLASTER WALL FINISH

REINF. CONCRETE SLAB

CONTINUOUS REINF. CONC. FOOTING

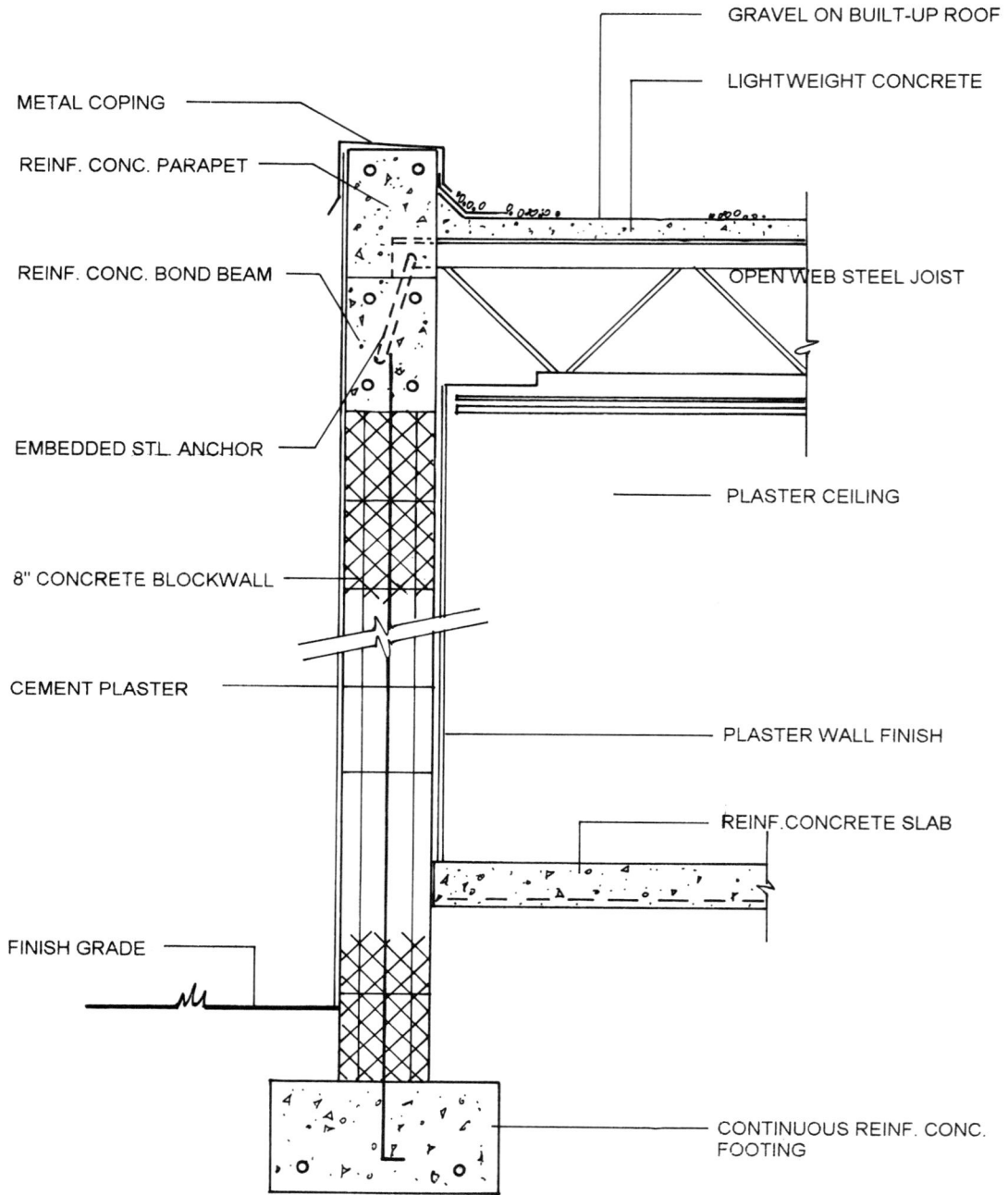

Typical section through an exterior block wall—commercial structure.

The foundation, whether wood post, piling, concrete piers, or footing walls under slabs, must be securely anchored (fastened) to the ground, and the superstructure must be anchored to the foundations. In other words, the whole structure must be anchored to the ground so that it will not float or blow off its foundation. Often wave action will wash out the sand underneath the slab poured directly on the ground, removing the structure's support and resulting in failure.

A structure must be built of materials that are tough and ductile to resist shock and impact. Wood, steel, and reinforced concrete are good. Hollow masonry, brick, and precast concrete panels are poor unless adequately reinforced and anchored.

Wood Structures

Wood is one of the best materials for absorbing short-duration loads such as those caused by wind. Whether or not the building will survive a storm, however, depends on how well the components are connected and how solid the anchoring is to the ground. A wood-frame house properly braced with well-fastened connections is hard to beat for safety against lateral forces such as wind or earthquakes.

The framing and sheathing of a wood-frame house should be nailed together using to good nailing practice (see Table 3 in Appendix C). Nailing should be supplemented by additional anchoring and reinforcing with metal straps, plates, and bolts, which strengthen the connections between the components of the frame. This will significantly improve the strength of the house at very little added cost. The basic principle is to ensure that the footing is tied to the foundation, the foundation to the floor, the floor to the walls, and the walls to the roof.

Bracing

A wood-frame building is most likely to suffer damage when it has insufficient lateral bracing or inadequate connections between lateral bracing and other structural elements. Lateral bracing may consist of shear walls of plywood or a series of lumber strips or metal straps at about a 45° angle across the studs. A shear wall is one that, in its own plane, provides resistance to racking forces from the action of wind on the adjoining walls at right angles to it. Racking (lateral or sideways collapse) occurs when the strain or deformation levels are beyond the norm. To prevent this, lumber diagonals should be made of 1×6's long enough to reach from the top plate (horizontal beam supporting the roof) to the sill (horizontal beam immediately above the foundation) at a 45° angle. The 1×6's should be nailed to each of the studs, the top plate, and the sill. Two cross-diagonals (X-bracing) are stronger than single diagonals.

An alternative to 1×6 lumber for diagonal bracing is a special steel strap 1 to 1.25 inches (2.5 to 3 cm) wide with holes for nailing to the top plate, sill, and each stud where they intersect, just as with the wood. For either type of bracing the minimum size of the nail should be 8d; 10d is preferable. The metal strap may often be easier to use for reinforcing an existing house.

The best alternative is shear-wall bracing—a continuous cover of plywood paneling over the studs. Where possible, extend the panels from the top plate to the sill. If the ceiling is too high for the usual 4 × 8-foot (1.2 × 2.4-m) plywood panel, use two panels of equal length instead of one 8-foot panel with a fill-in of a few inches. The edges of the paneling should be nailed securely with nails at least 8d in size at 6-inch (15-cm) centers. The intermediate nailing of panel to stud can be at 12-inch (30-cm) centers. The plywood should be ½ inch (1.3 cm) thick.

Rafter Construction

The use of steel plates to strengthen the connections between members is highly recommended. Collar ties should be provided between opposite rafters on the two sides of the roof underneath the ridge. This can be a 1 × 6-inch or a 2 × 4-inch collar beam (the horizontal base of a triangle) or a plywood gusset.

DESIGN OF BUILDINGS IN EARTHQUAKE AREAS

A severe earthquake always leaves in its wake many collapsed buildings and much structural damage. Reports on earthquake disasters show that a properly designed structure is capable of withstanding the strongest recorded shocks.

Earthquakes are natural phenomena that occur frequently in certain regions of the world, but although the earth's surface is shaken by tremors hundreds of thousands of times each year, relatively few are intense enough to damage buildings. The zones of major risk form a belt extending from the American Pacific coast, across Japan, East China, Indonesia, and the Middle East to the Mediterranean and are largely situated in the tropics. Some countries are located entirely in earthquake areas, while others are divided into three or four probable zones.

Whatever the basic cause, an earthquake usually originates some (16,400–328,000 feet) (5–100 km) below the surface of the earth; the place or line where this happens is called the *focus*. The point on the surface immediately above the focus is referred to as the *epicenter*. The sudden rupture at the focus of an earthquake causes horizontal and vertical vibrations to go out in all directions in the form of waves, which are reflected in different ways by the various materials of the earth's crust, causing an unpredictable and complicated pattern. The horizontal motion is usually much greater than the vertical motion, the latter being one-tenth to one-fifth of the former. Vertical vibrations are generally so small that they may be disregarded.

The most destructive force is caused by horizontal earth motion. When the ground underneath a structure is moved suddenly to one side, the building tends to remain in its original position because of inertia. The foundation will move back and forth with the ground. These vibrations can be quite intense, creating stresses and deformations throughout the structure. Flexible structures, such as frame buildings without shear wall-stiffening elements, will endure large deflections, often with extensive nonstructural damage. Load-bearing concrete masonry buildings, on the other hand, are much stiffer than frame building and resist deflection. Nonstructural damage is minimized, as well as the hazard from falling debris. Unlike many buildings, which concentrate lateral loads to each wall, load-bearing walls minimize force concentration, which reduces torsional twisting of the structure.

In general, buildings should be designed to resist lateral forces in any direction because an earthquake may occur in any direction. The earth's movement, however, can be replaced by two components acting parallel to the axis of the building; therefore, it is sufficient to investigate the structure's strength in two perpendicular directions. Before attempting an earthquake design, the local building code should be referred to for guidelines.

Two approaches to earthquake design are presented. The *basic strategy* is to construct a very strong building and attach it securely to the ground. This strategy has not changed and will be discussed first. An alternative method has finally reached the application stage. This is *base isolation,* which involves detaching the building from the ground in such a way that the earthquake's motion is not transmitted up through the building or at least is greatly reduced. This approach will be discussed afterwards.

To illustrate the effect of earthquakes on buildings, the accompanying figure shows a house set above the ground on piers. The bottoms of these piers must move with the ground, and the tendency is to transmit the motion to the building above. The sudden change from rest to motion causes forces (inertia reactions) to act on the superstructure opposite to the earth's movement. The building is loaded, and the different elements of the structure are stressed in a manner similar to that of a cantilever beam. To provide for these stresses is the purpose of an earthquake design.

The building in this figure is toppling over because the connection between the superstructure and the top of the piers failed to transmit the lateral forces. A continuous foundation wall is preferable to piers since the forces that tend to move the building off its foundation are not concentrated at a few isolated points.

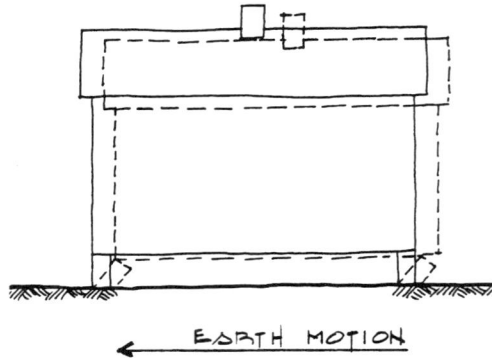

Effect of earthquake on a house on piers.

For convenience, it should be assumed that the lateral forces are applied at different floor levels as indicated in the accompanying figure. The lateral forces must be registered either by the walls or by the framing system. Partitions and outside walls parallel to the direction of the earth's movement (cross walls) possess much greater strength and rigidity against distortion than those normal to this direction. Moreover, cross walls generally possess greater rigidity than frames extending in the same direction and will absorb practically all the lateral forces.

All parts of a building should be firmly tied together and so stiffly braced that the building will tend to move as a unit. Floors and cross walls should be continuous throughout the building, and openings should, if possible, be away from outside corners.

It is desirable for the height of a building to be uniform. In planning a design, a closed shape, preferably square or nearly square, is pre-

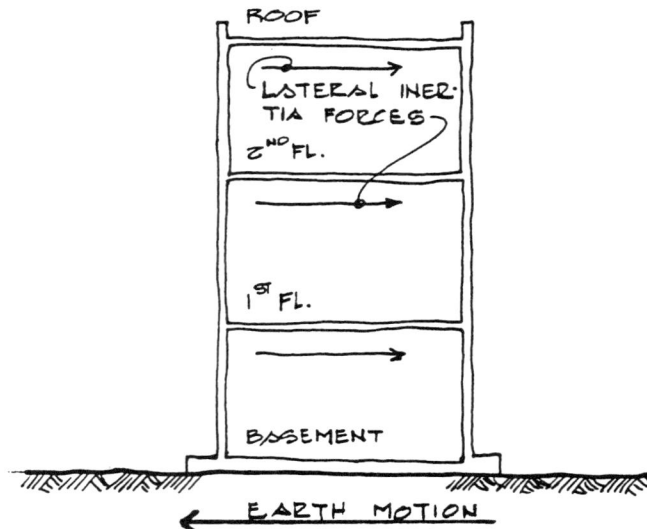

Lateral forces due to the earth's motion.

SECTION X-X

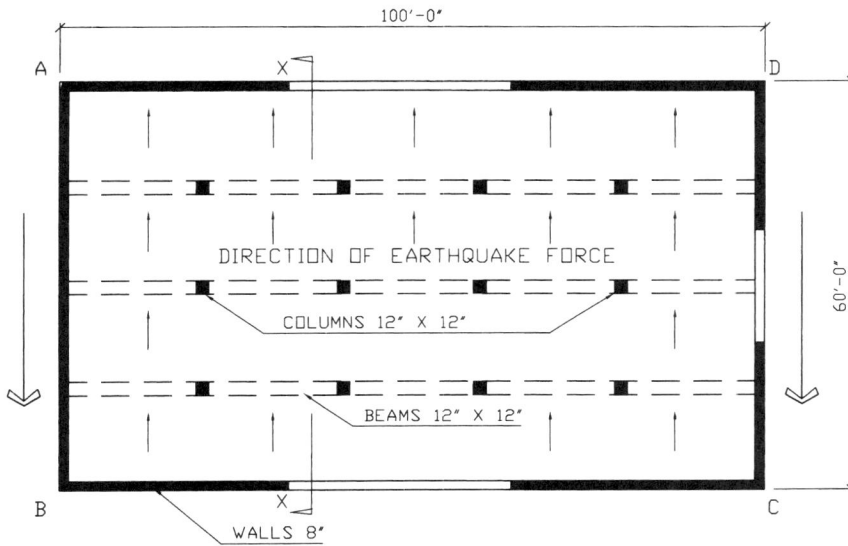

Diaphragm action of a floor slab.

100'-0"

A   X   D

DIRECTION OF EARTHQUAKE FORCE

COLUMNS 12" X 12"

BEAMS 12" X 12"

60'-0"

B   X   C

WALLS 8"

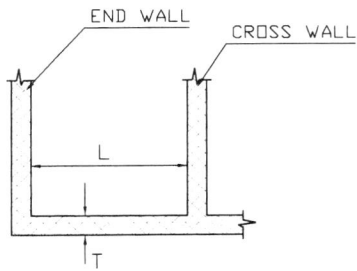

END WALL   CROSS WALL

L

T

CROSS OR END WALLS

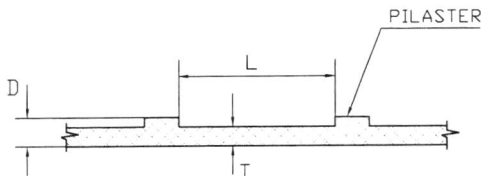

ROOF

FLOOR

FLOOR

Vertical supports.

HORIZ. SUPPORTS

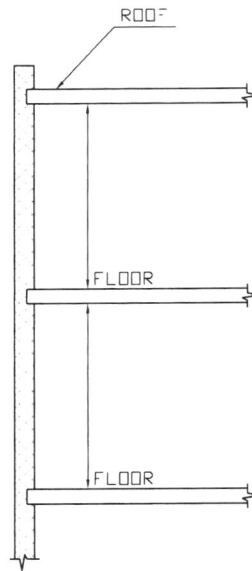

PILASTER

D   L

T

PIERS OR BUTTRESSES

Typical vertical supports.

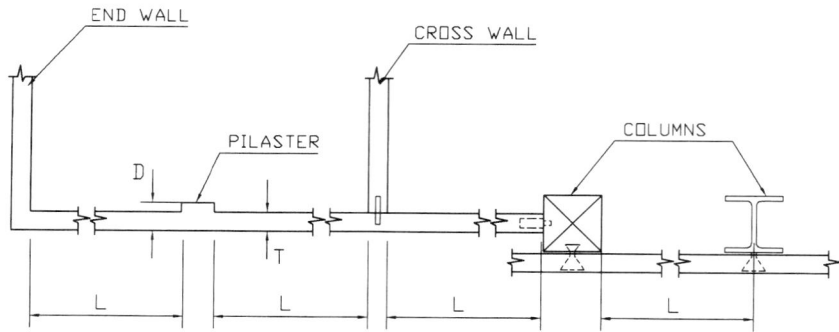

ferred because these shapes lend themselves most easily to symmetrical bracing. However, asymmetrically shaped buildings may be built to withstand earthquakes, provided that they are properly designed.

Adjacent buildings or parts of the same building dissimilar in mass or stiffness should be sufficiently separated to prevent them from pounding one another during an earthquake because of different rates of movement. This can be accomplished with special joints, sometimes called "crumple sections" that allow a total movement of 6 to 8 inches in all directions. Stucco ¾″ thick or some other easily material may be used. The accompanying figure shows an arrangement of these special joints for a group of buildings or for a building with large wings. The separation should be carried down to the top of the foundation, which may be continuous for an entire group of buildings.

Separation of adjoining buildings.

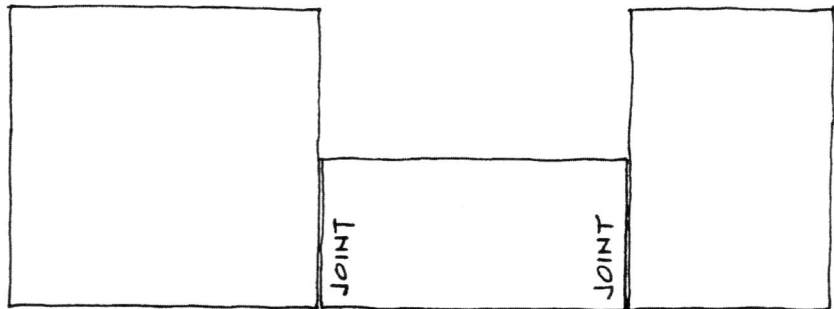

Base Isolation

Base isolation has required much research to make it feasible, and only with modern computer analysis has it become possible. The first patten for such a system was recorded in England in 1909. Base isolation works primarily by two methods. One is designed for a single, large, controlled lateral movement (or drift) at the building base rather than allowing drift throughout the height of the building. The

Lateral distortion of a building.

other method is to "detune" the building, making its natural period of vibration different from that of the ground beneath so that amplification will not occur. Base isolation achieves detuning by lengthening the natural period of the building so that it moves slowly while the ground beneath vibrates more rapidly. The building above the isolator is designed to be stiff so that, as it moves back and forth, the energy of the earthquake is dissipated in the bearings that attach the building to the ground rather than moving through the building itself.

For the bearing to absorb the energy of the earthquake, some unusual properties are necessary. The bearing must be strong in compression, for it must support the weight of the building and yet be able to accommodate large lateral movements. Spring, for example, allows large lateral deflections but does not automatically provide a returning force, so that once the building starts to move laterally, it tends to continue moving.

Many concepts meant to achieve base isolation have been studied. They include schemes incorporating torsion bars, similar to those used in automobile suspensions, to introduce energy dissipation and damping. A new system now being tested uses ball bearing-type supports in shaped housings that automatically introduce increased damping forces as the building moves. The most highly developed bearings so far are those that use natural rubber laminated with steel, sometimes with lead introduced as a damping agent.

One completed project with base isolation uses rubber/steel/lead bearings and another uses a torsion bar system. Nuclear power plants have been constructed using a rubber and steel system developed in France.

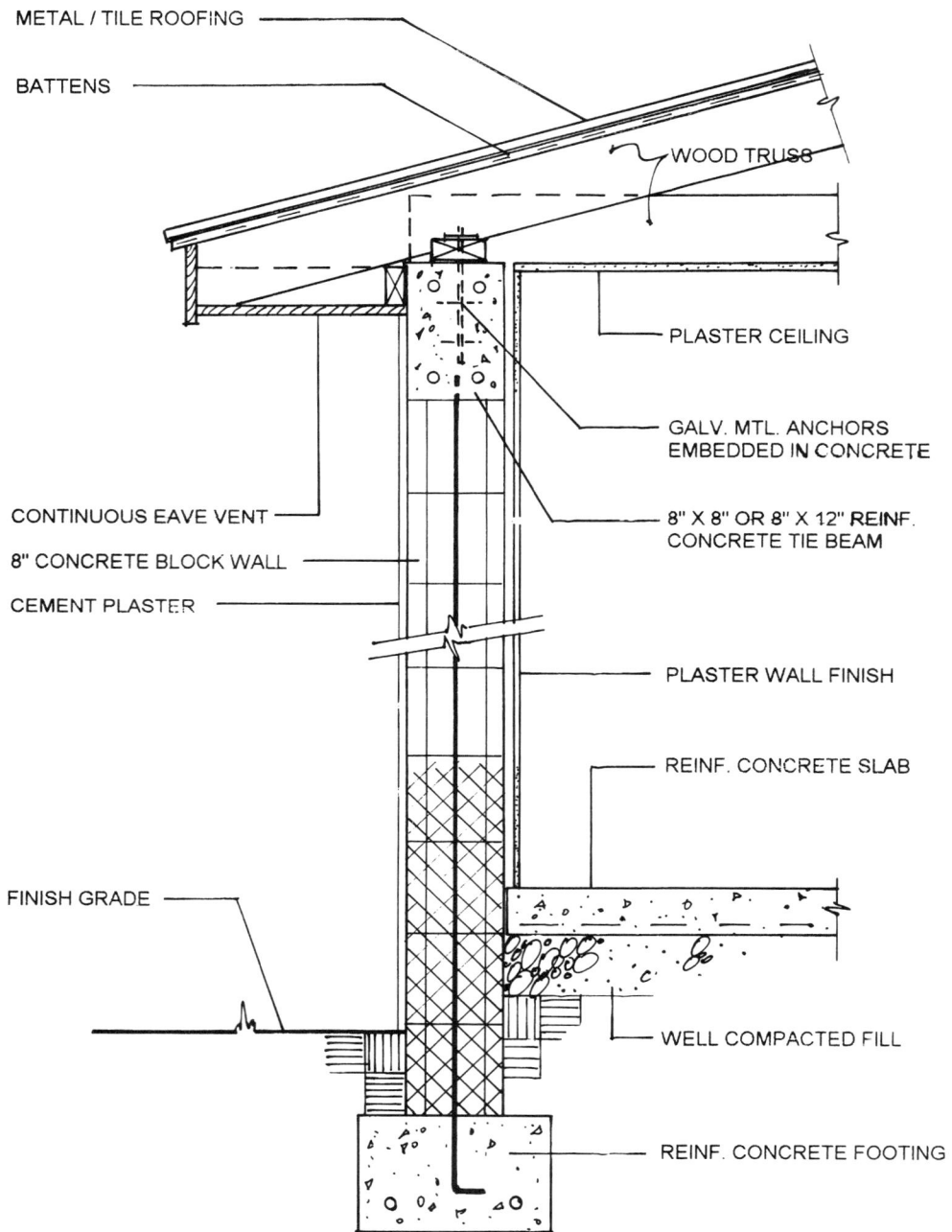

METAL / TILE ROOFING

BATTENS

WOOD TRUSS

PLASTER CEILING

GALV. MTL. ANCHORS
EMBEDDED IN CONCRETE

CONTINUOUS EAVE VENT

8" CONCRETE BLOCK WALL

CEMENT PLASTER

8" X 8" OR 8" X 12" REINF.
CONCRETE TIE BEAM

PLASTER WALL FINISH

REINF. CONCRETE SLAB

FINISH GRADE

WELL COMPACTED FILL

REINF. CONCRETE FOOTING

Typical section through an exterior block wall—residential structure.

166

RECOMMENDATIONS FOR TROPICAL CLIMATE ZONES

Warm-Wet to Hot-Wet Zones

Climate Summary

> High rainfall and high humidity
>
> Low diurnal range
>
> relatively high and even temperature throughout the year
>
> Light winds and long periods of still air
>
> High radiation intensity with strong sky glare.
>
> Rainfall usually in the afternoon, often accompanied by violent electric storms

Problems and Requirements

The climate creates uncomfortably hot, sticky conditions that require high air velocity past the body to increase sweat evaporation throughout the year. Buildings require mainly openness and shading. They must be designed to provide continuous, efficient ventilation and protection from sun, rain, and insects. Structures may need to withstand hurricane-velocity winds, and in certain cases, safe shelters may be necessary for the hurricane period. Termites can be a problem.

Response: General

Layout and Form: Buildings should be separated and scattered, with free spaces between them to utilize air flow. Individual structures should be freely elongated and rooms preferably single banked, with access from open verandahs or galleries. It may be advantageous to raise buildings on stilts.

Orientation: North and south for habitable rooms, but if buildings are in shade, variation is possible to provide maximum air flow. Orientation to reduce solar radiation is most important with high-rise buildings.

Rooms: Ideally, rooms have openings on both the windward and leeward sides. Heat- and moisture-producing areas should be isolated and ventilated separately.

Outdoor Areas: Like buildings, outdoor areas should be shaded, and vegetation must not block free passage of air. Adequate storm water drainage must be provided.

Response: Structure

Windows and Ventilation: Openings should be large, with inlets of similar size where a wide spread of air is needed. Large sliding doors or folding walls and adjustable louvers are commonly used.

Screens, lattices, grills, and so on are useful to admit air and provide protection against glare. Flyscreens are essential; they also reduce air flow, so they should should be installed away from windows (e.g., around a verandah or balcony). Openings must be protected from radiation, glare, driving rain, and noise.

Walls: Walls have less thermal value than in any other zone. Lightweight construction materials with low thermal capacity is recommended. The height of walls should be kept down to make it easier to shade them and protect them from rain. Unshaded walls must be insulated and have a reflective outer surface.

Roof: The roof should be pitched to shed rain, with a wide overhang for protection against glare, direct sunlight, and driving rain. It should be constructed from lightweight, low thermal capacity materials. A well-ventilated double roof is preferable, but it must be able to withstand strong winds. Ceilings should be well insulated and covered with a reflective upper surface. The space between the roof and the ceiling should be treated and protected against insects, rodents, and so on.

Surfaces: The roof and exposed walls should be reflective (light colored). It is difficult, however, to maintain light-colored paints in this climate because of high humidity and fungal growth.

Tropical Marine Areas

In warm-humid island zones the sun is lower in the sky, so solar radiation will be more intense on the wall facing the equator. Extra care is needed to protect this wall. Winds are constant and in some areas even predictable, but hurricanes present a hazard.

Hot-Dry Zones

Climate Summary

    Hot, sunny, direct solar radiation and high reflectivity

    High diurnal and annual temperature ranges

    Low humidity and precipitation

    Sandy environment with dust storms

    Climate generally healthier than those of warm-humid lands

Problems and Requirements

Uncomfortable conditions are created by extremes of heat and dryness. Sand and dust storms are a nuisance. Buildings must be adapted to summer conditions; basically, this means providing protection from intense radiation from the sun, ground, and surrounding buildings. Reduction of heat takes precedence over air movement during daytime. Measures must be taken to reduce glare and prevent dust penetration.

Response: General

Layout and Form: Compact planning for groups of buildings is required to provide mutual shading and minimum exposure. Enclosed, compactly planned, inward-looking buildings are most suitable; patios and courtyards are advisable. For large buildings, high, cubical, and massive forms are advantageous.

Orientation: Larger dimensions and windows should face north and south. The worst orientation, west-east, can be used for non-habitable spaces to form a thermal barrier.

Rooms: Rooms can be deep and ideally should open on to a patio or indoor courtyard. Heat-producing areas should be isolated and ventilated separately.

Outdoor Areas: Outdoor areas must be enclosed, inward looking, contain plants, be cooled by water, and be shaded for most of the day. Paved surfaces should be avoided wherever possible. Provision must be made for outdoor sleeping.

Response: Structure

Windows and Ventilation: Windows should be relatively small, particularly on outside walls, and must be shielded from direct radiation and glare. Ventilation during the day must be kept to a minimum for hygienic reasons; good ventilation is required at night.

Walls: The simplest solution is to follow tradition and use the thickest suitable walls. Rooms used only in the evenings can be of materials with low heat-retaining capacity that cool quickly after sunset.

Roof: Roofing materials should be solid and heat storing, with a reflective upper surface; flat concrete roofs are often used. Water spray or a pool on the roof can be effective. A double roof is sometimes used. The inner layer is heavy, with a reflective upper surface. The outer layer is lightweight, with a highly reflective surface above and a low emittance surface below. There is a ventilated air space between the two layers.

Surfaces: A whitewash finish is the cheapest, simplest, and most effective way of making outer surfaces reflective; these surfaces must be frequently repainted. Light colors can cause glare off walls; a light brown color is sometimes used.

Maritime Zones

Maritime zones are similar to hot-dry zones, but their higher humidity causes discomfort; humidity tends to reduce diurnal variations and moderate temperatures. Air movement is required at all times, so high-thermal-capacity structures are not as effective. Wind towers a very effective in these zones. A lightweight area catching the breeze for daytime use is ideal.

Cool-Cold Dry (Subtropical) Zones

Climate Summary

Warm to hot, dry summers

Cool winters with moderate rainfall

Intense solar radiation, especially in summer

Large variation in temperature, humidity, and rainfall, depending on the location (e.g., marine, continental, or mountainous)

Diurnal range large in continental locations and small in marine locations

Problems and Requirements

Buildings must be designed to provide protection from summer heat and from cold and rain in winter. In continental locations, summer heat and dust create problems similar to those found in hot-dry zones; in maritime locations, heat and humidity in summer require good ventilation. Condensation can be a problem in winter in marine locations. Dust can be a problem in summer, particularly in continental areas. Some heating in winter is usually necessary.

Response: General

Layout and Form: In continental areas, the requirements are similar to those in hot-dry lands, but because the climate is more moderate, spacing need not be so compact to allow for sun and light in winter. Courtyards are suitable. In marine areas, buildings on an east-west axis, with adequate spacing to allow for breeze penetration, are more appropriate.

Orientation: Because of the intense solar radiation, windows should face north and south, but prevailing breezes must be considered in marine locations.

Rooms: Room should preferably be single banked in marine areas; if they are double banked adequately, provision must be made for good air flow.

Outdoor Spaces: Courtyards are useful for shade in summer and protection from cold winds in winter in continental locations. Shaded areas can utilize breezes in marine areas, but protection against winter winds must be kept in mind.

Response: Structure

Windows and Ventilation: In continental areas the requirements are similar to those in hot-dry lands but with cold winters, sun is welcome during this period. Medium-sized openings are needed to ensure good air flow during summer and permit the penetration of sun in winter.

Walls: In continental areas, the requirements are the same as those for hot-dry zones. In marine areas, heat capacity is not as important, but internal walls and floors should be heavy to store heat during winter while preventing the internal temperature from rising too much when sun is allowed to penetrate through windows.

Roof: A sloping roof is required to shed rain. It should provide shade for windows and protection from rain. Otherwise, the requirements are the same as for hot-dry zones.

Surfaces: The walls and roof should be reflective (light-colored) where not shaded.

Subtropical Humid Zone

This is a complex climate from the designer's point of view. Basically, the same response is required as for warm-humid zones, but provision must be made for the winter months, which can be cold.

Composite Zones

Climate Summary

> Two or three distinct seasons, one similar to that of hot-dry deserts (usually longest period) and another similar to that of the the warm-wet zones.
>
> A third season in some places—cool and dry, with low humidity, warm sunny days, and cold nights
>
> Diurnal range large during dry seasons and small during wet periods
>
> Variation in radiation and direction of glare, depending on the season

Problems and Requirements

Composite zones are complex climates from the designers's point of view. Buildings must satisfy conflicting needs of the hot-dry and warm-humid periods and must, in some places, provide for a cool or cold season. Where incompatible needs arise, the length, duration, and relative severity of seasons must be analyzed to find a balanced solution and the most satisfactory compromise. Mahoney tables would be useful for assessing the requirements; a study of local building traditions is also helpful.

Response: General

Layout and Form: With conflicting requirements, different solutions may be equally appropriate. The layout should be moderately compact to provide mutual shading and shelter from wind in the cold season but allow prevailing breezes to be used in the humid period.

Courtyard buildings are suitable; terraced buildings facing north and south may also be appropriate.

Orientation: Buildings should be oriented north and south, but prevailing breezes during the humid period must be considered, as well as radiation requirements in cold months.

Rooms: If rooms are double banked, adequate internal openings must be provided to ensure good air flow during the humid period.

Outdoor Spaces: The courtyard is a most pleasant space for most of the year if shaded during the hot period and sunny during the cool months; a pergola with a deciduous creeper is one solution. Provision for outdoor sleeping may be essential.

Response: Structure

Windows and Ventilation: Medium-sized openings are required in opposite walls, but with thick shutters to reduce the flow of heat and dusty air during the hot, dry season (opened in evenings) and cold air in the cool season. Provision must be made for ventilation during these periods; the simplest solution is one high-level opening and one low-level opening. Wind towers are sometimes used, with the catcher opening covered during cold weather. Windows must be protected from radiation and glare (from both sky and ground), but shading is undesirable in winter.

Walls: Thick, heavy walls are required for hot-dry and cold periods. However, because large openings are needed in the outer walls, thermal capacity should be provided through heavy internal walls, floors, and ceilings. In hot seasons, walls should be shaded and surfaces exposed to sun should be light colored. In cold periods, sun is required on walls.

Roof: A heavy roof with a reflective outer surface is necessary. Large projecting eaves are advisable for shade and for protection against glare and rain.

Surface: Surfaces exposed to the sun during the hot and warm seasons should be light colored or of shiny metal. Some of the surfaces receiving sun during the cold (but not the hot) season should be absorptive.

Uplands

Upland (or highland) zones, although having more moderate temperatures, are dominated by strong solar radiation; adequate shading for windows and outdoor activities in summer is therefore important. The roof is very important, as it receives the greatest amount of radiation. Nights can become cold, and some heating may have to be provided for winter.

Case Studies

CASE STUDY 1

Proposed School of Architecture
University of the West Indies, Mona Campus
St. Andrew, Jamaica

The design calls for the School of architecture to be Caribbean in both source and execution, utilizing as much locally found and manufactured materials and construction techniques as possible. The basic philosophy of the school is to integrate a variety of disciplines: fine arts, freehand exercises, and technical training with building design and planning. This will not only give architects a strong command of the elements of the architectural profession but will also exhibit the essence of design.

Orientation is a primary consideration in the school's design, taking advantage of prevailing winds and natural lighting to provide passive solar energy. The architectural style adapted is appropriate to the place and purpose and has been chosen to blend with the

Site plan—proposed school of architecture.

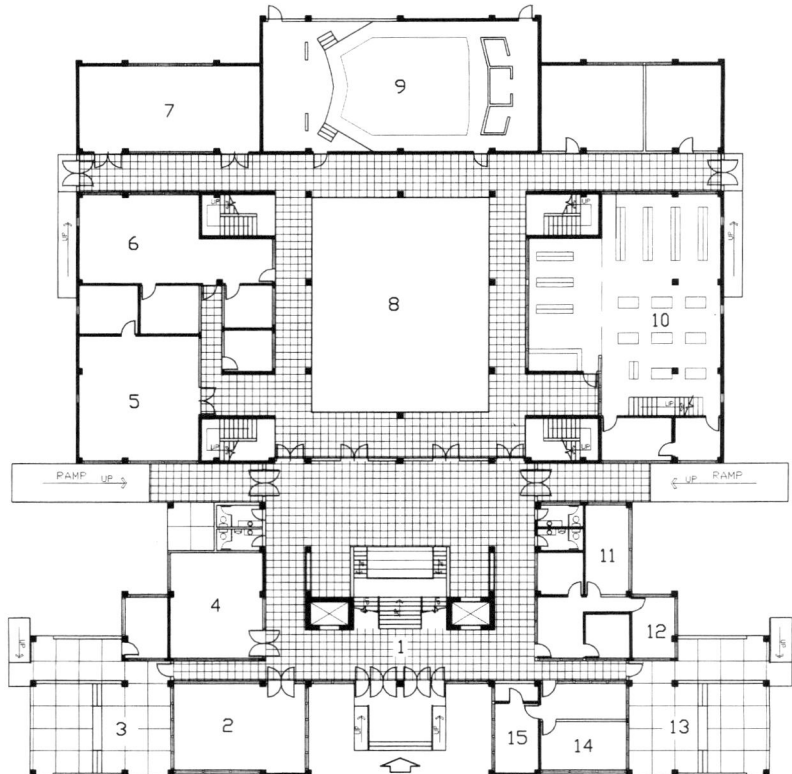

Ground-floor plan.

1	LOBBY	9	LECTURE HALL
2	MAIN GALLERY	10	LIBRARY
3	EATING	11	STAFF LOUNGE
4	GALLERY	12	CHAIRMAN
5	FREEHAND EXERCISE	13	PATIO
6	SCULPTURE & MODEL	14	CONFERENCE ROOM
7	STUDENT COMMON	15	DEAN
8	OUTDOOR COURTYARD		

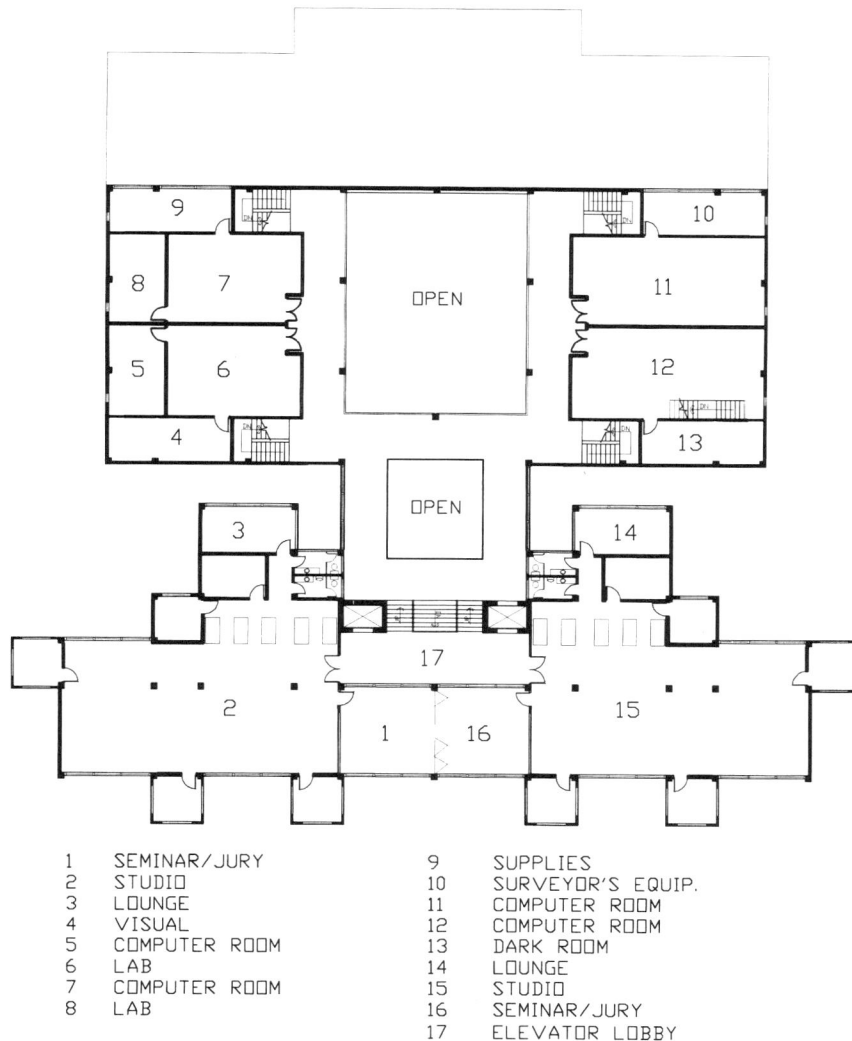

First-floor plan.

1	SEMINAR/JURY	9	SUPPLIES
2	STUDIO	10	SURVEYOR'S EQUIP.
3	LOUNGE	11	COMPUTER ROOM
4	VISUAL	12	COMPUTER ROOM
5	COMPUTER ROOM	13	DARK ROOM
6	LAB	14	LOUNGE
7	COMPUTER ROOM	15	STUDIO
8	LAB	16	SEMINAR/JURY
		17	ELEVATOR LOBBY

environment, while making a contemporary architectural statement. As a place of higher learning, it will look like a college built in a tropical setting. Its materials have been chosen to reflect the attitude of both the school's users and the elements of the existing campus. Skylights and operable high-level windows are provided to promote natural ventilation. Developing the classroom block and circulation around interior courtyards increases natural ventilation and lighting.

An extension of the community is suggested by means of the landscape treatment, views, and forms adopted. The development of the total environment around the school will be given special consid-

Second-floor plan.

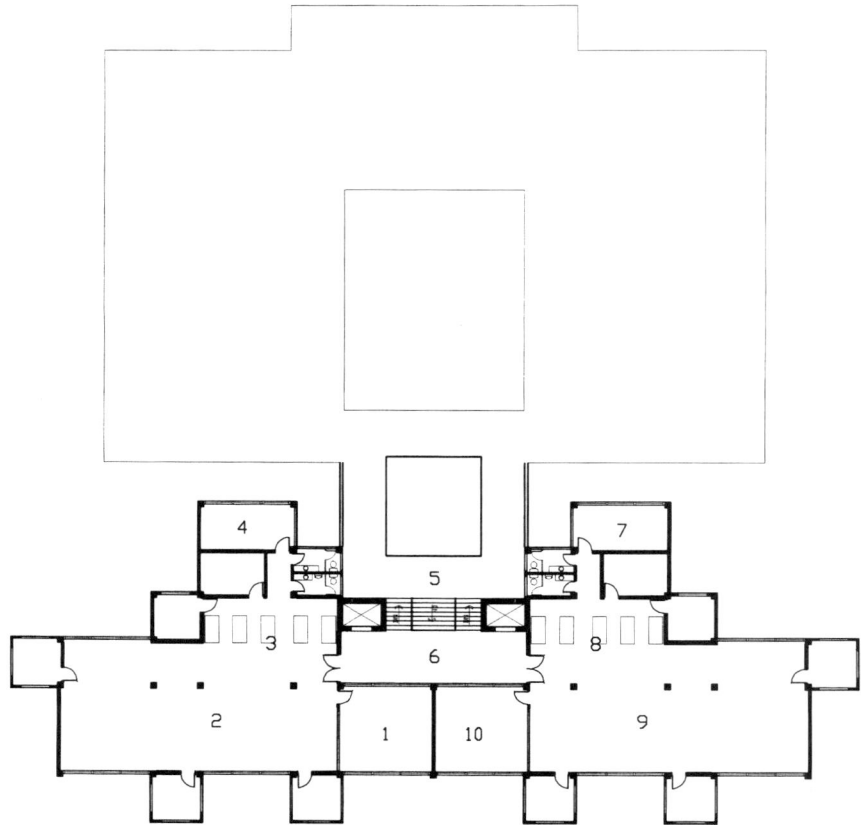

1	SEMINAR	6	ELEVATOR LOBBY
2	STUDIO	7	LOUNGE
3	CUTTING AREA	8	CUTTING AREA
4	LOUNGE	9	STUDIO
5	MEZZANINE LEVEL	10	SEMINAR

1 LOBBY
2 SEMINAR/JURY CORE
3 SEMINAR
4 BALCONY
5 LECTURE HALL
6 OUTDOOR COURTYARD
7 INTERIOR COURTYARD

Section A-A.

eration; landscaping, both hard and soft, will be tasteful but simple. This will provide fluidity between the existing campus and the new building.

CASE STUDY 2

Strawberry Hill   1995
Irish Town
St. Andrew, Jamaica

The original Strawberry Hill Great House, built in the late 1700s, was severely damaged in 1989 by Hurricane Gilbert and replaced with a series of small cottages, restaurant, and administrative and recreational buildings nestled in the Blue Mountains located 3,100 feet above Kingston. The complex also includes a small conference room to accommodate thirty people, as well as a sixteen-seat board-room with the latest in audiovisual equipment.

The naturally landscaped site provides the perfect setting for an architecture and land-use plan that conserves the natural terrain and is one with nature. The design, the materials used, and the method of construction show sensitivity to both the site and the climate, integrating environmentally sensitive architecture into the serene hillside plantation. Landscaping in the form of shrubs and fully grown canopy trees is utilized to provide shade from the sun and pri-

Office and Administrative Buildings 1995
Strawberry Hill
Near Irish Town
St. Andrew, Jamaica

**Restaurant and Meeting
Rooms   1995
Strawberry Hill
Near Irish Town
St. Andrew, Jamaica**

**View of Blue Mountains
from Verandah   1995
Strawberry Hill
Near Irish Town
St. Andrew, Jamaica**

vacy. The simplicity of the layout, responding to the natural contours of the site, and the relationship of the cottages to both the public spaces and the surrounding add to its success.

The Strawberry Hill resort was developed in response to the new trend in providing small specialized resorts, centered on unique recreational activities, in close proximity to local cultural attractions.

Typical Cottage   1995
Strawberry Hill
Near Irish Town
St. Andrew, Jamaica

Typical Cottage   1995
Strawberry Hill
Near Irish Town
St. Andrew, Jamaica

View along Verandah   1995
Strawberry Hill
Near Irish Town
St. Andrew, Jamaica

CASE STUDY 3

Honolulu Academy of Arts   1927
900 South Beretania Street
Honolulu, Oahu

The Honolulu Academy of Arts is a regional design with many residential qualities. The building has a massive tile Hawaiian roof, a shaded entrance arcade, textured masonry exteriors, and an Oriental pavilion interior plan. Gallery rooms are oriented around five landscaped open courts, including the Asian Court and the Mediterranean Court. The building is of architectural interest because of the extensive use of local materials such as lava rock, sandstone from Moloka'i, and recycled granite pavers and Chinese glazed grilles salvaged from razed buildings.

ROBERT ALLERTON LIBRARY

SCULPTURE GARDEN

MEDITERRANEAN COURT

LUCE WING

SCULPTURE COURT

GARDEN CAFE

CENTRAL COURT

MEMBERSHIP DEPARTMENT

KINAU COURT

ACADEMY SHOP

ASIAN COURT

FOUNTAIN COURT GALLERY

FOUNTAIN COURT

EDUCATION DEPARTMENT

EDUCATION GALLERY

JOHN YOUNG GALLERY

WARD AVENUE ENTRANCE

BERETANIA STREET ENTRANCE

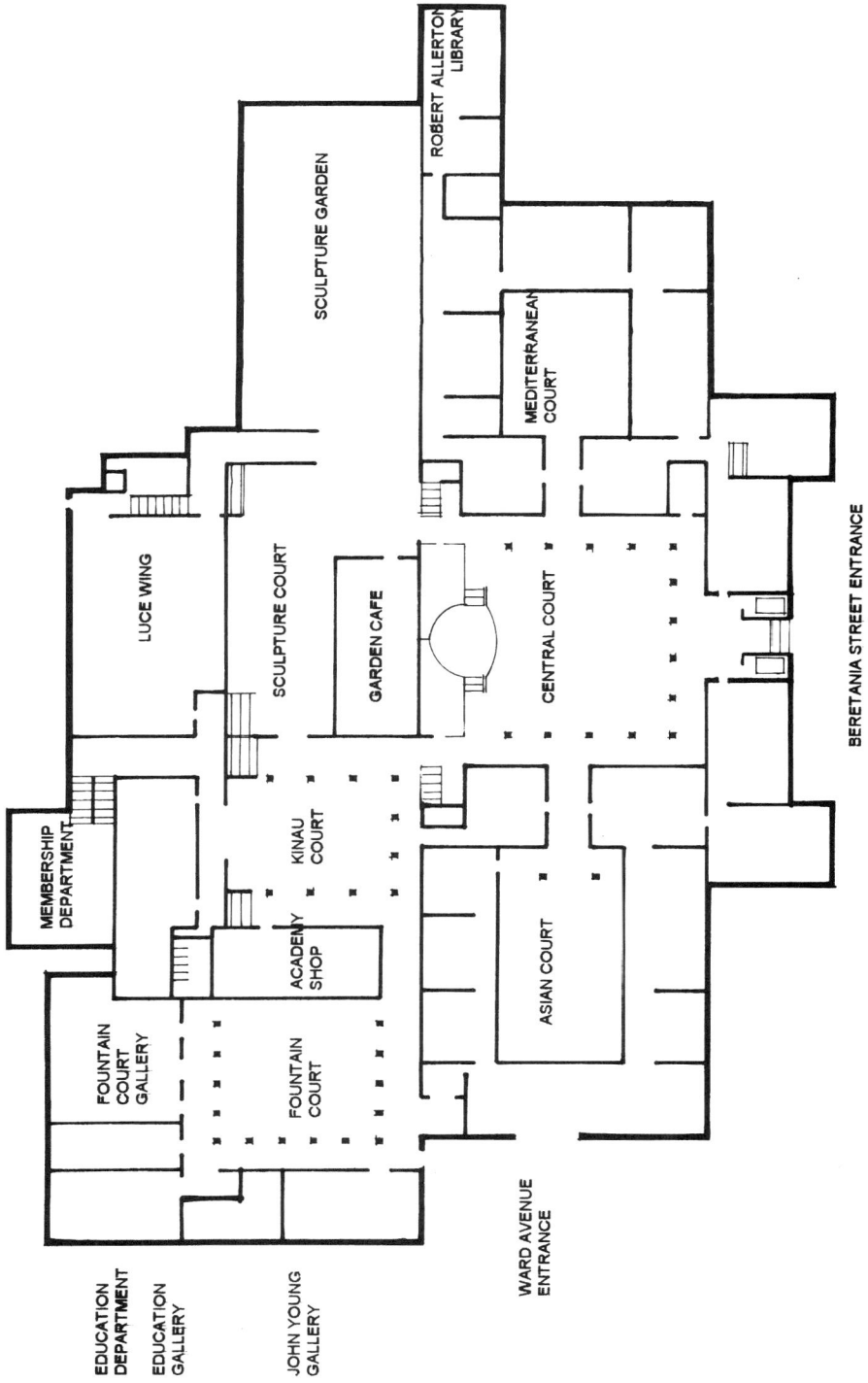

Floor plan—Honolulu Academy of Arts. (architect: Bertram Grosvenor Goodhue and Hardie Phillips).

181

Honolulu Academy of Arts   1927
900 South Beretania Street
Honolulu, Oahu

CASE STUDY 4

Sacramento's Justice Department Building
Sacramento, California
Van der Ryn (Architect)

The building's design philosophy relies heavily on passive technology, depending very little on artificial lighting and conventional air conditioning for cooling. The major design objectives were to reduce the peak heating and cooling loads, to shift as much of the energy consumption as possible to off-peak hours, to reduce total energy use, and to provide effective integration of the energy systems with the other architectural requirements of the building. In order to accomplish this, the architect designed two L-shaped, four-story sections clad in a tight building skin, shaded with operable exterior sunshades, and wrapped around a spacious covered skylit court. The interior courtyard, one of the key elements of the whole concept, is surrounded by balconies and galleries intended for social activities. It contains the main vertical and horizontal circulation for the building and two thermal storage rockbeds.

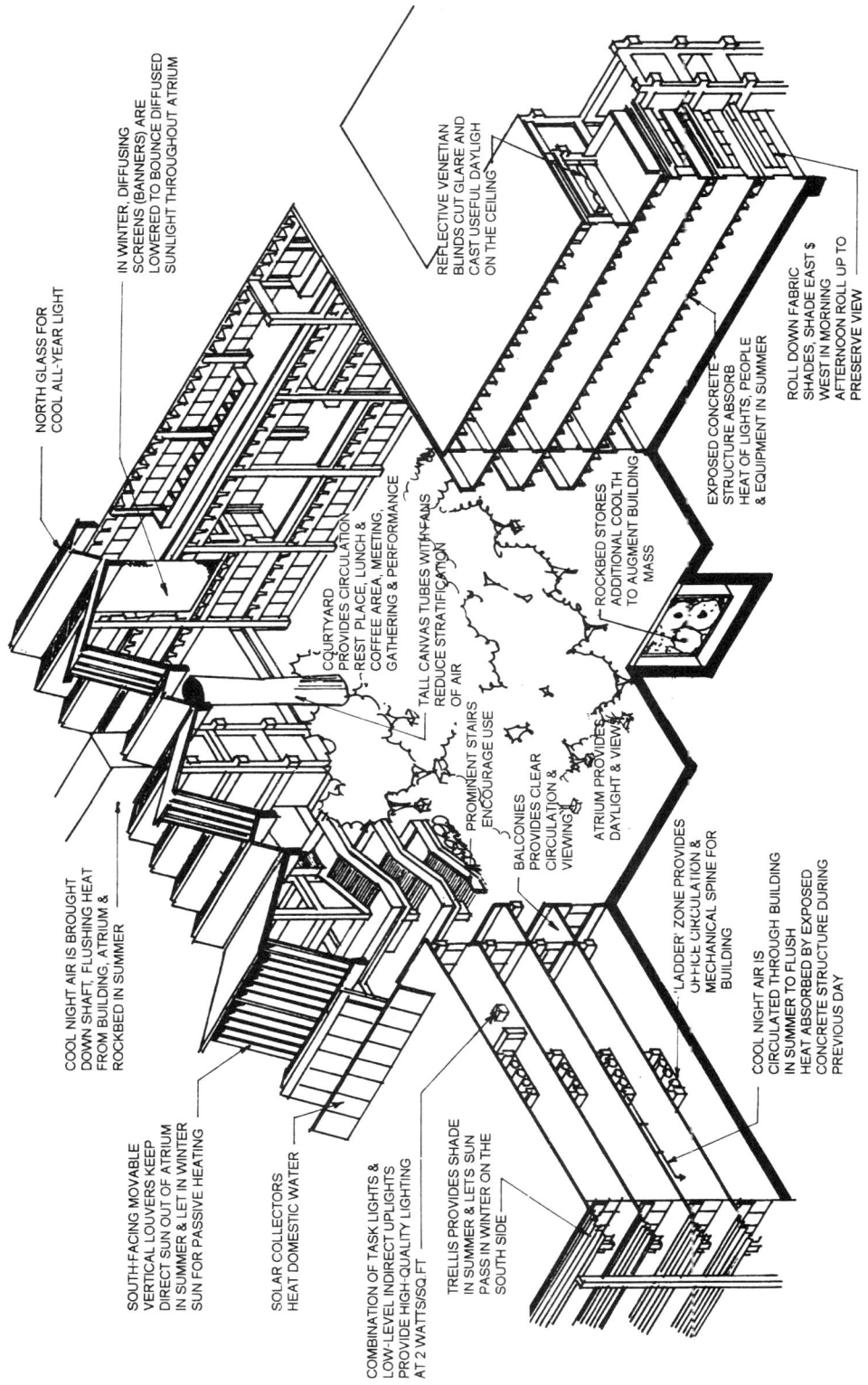

GENERAL:

. MOST WINTER HEATING LOADS ARE OFFSET BY HEAT FROM LIGHTS, PEOPLE & EQUIPMENT.
. 65% OF SUMMER COOLING IS HANDLED BY 'NIGHT VENTING'. THIS VENTING CIRCULATES SACRAMENTO'S TYPICAL COOL NIGHT AIR THROUGH THE BUILDING, LOWERING THE TEMPERATURE OF THE CONCRETE STRUCTURE & STORING THE 'COOLTH' FOR THE NEXT DAY. THE ROCKBED 'THERMAL BATTERY' MEETS 26% OF THE ANNUAL COOLING LOAD.

NORTH GLASS FOR COOL ALL-YEAR LIGHT

IN WINTER, DIFFUSING SCREENS (BANNERS) ARE LOWERED TO BOUNCE DIFFUSED SUNLIGHT THROUGHOUT ATRIUM

REFLECTIVE VENETIAN BLINDS CUT GLARE AND CAST DAYLIGH ON THE CEILING

ROLL DOWN FABRIC SHADES, SHADE EAST $ IN MORNING AFTERNOON ROLL UP TO PRESERVE VIEW

EXPOSED CONCRETE STRUCTURE ABSORB HEAT OF LIGHTS, PEOPLE & EQUIPMENT IN SUMMER

ROCKBED STORES ADDITIONAL COOLTH TO AUGMENT BUILDING MASS

COURTYARD PROVIDES CIRCULATION REST PLACE, LUNCH & COFFEE AREA, MEETING, GATHERING & PERFORMANCE

TALL CANVAS TUBES WITH FANS REDUCE STRATIFICATION OF AIR

ATRIUM PROVIDES DAYLIGHT & VIEWS

PROMINENT STAIRS ENCOURAGE USE

BALCONIES PROVIDES CLEAR CIRCULATION & VIEWING

'LADDER' ZONE PROVIDES OFFICE CIRCULATION & MECHANICAL SPINE FOR BUILDING

COOL NIGHT AIR IS CIRCULATED THROUGH BUILDING IN SUMMER TO FLUSH HEAT ABSORBED BY EXPOSED CONCRETE STRUCTURE DURING PREVIOUS DAY

COOL NIGHT AIR IS BROUGHT DOWN SHAFT, FLUSHING HEAT FROM BUILDING, ATRIUM & ROCKBED IN SUMMER

SOUTH-FACING MOVABLE VERTICAL LOUVERS KEEP DIRECT SUN OUT OF ATRIUM IN SUMMER & LET IN WINTER SUN FOR PASSIVE HEATING

SOLAR COLLECTORS HEAT DOMESTIC WATER

COMBINATION OF TASK LIGHTS & LOW-LEVEL INDIRECT UPLIGHTS PROVIDE HIGH-QUALITY LIGHTING AT 2 WATTS/SQ FT

TRELLIS PROVIDES SHADE IN SUMMER & LETS SUN PASS IN WINTER ON THE SOUTH SIDE

Justice Department Building—Sacramento, California. (architect: Sim Van der Ryn). (Reprinted from the 2nd National Passive Solar Conference Proceedings, March 16–18, 1978, with permission from the American Solar Energy Society)

183

The reinforced concrete structure and a large rockbed act as a thermal storage mass that is cooled by the ocean breeze blowing up from the San Francisco Bay, causing daytime temperatures to drop by up to 35°F. Vents are carefully positioned to trap the breeze, which is drawn through the building during the day by fans. This causes the hot daytime air to be expelled, relying on the mechanical air-conditioning system only as a backup under extreme circumstances.

A Regional Photographic Tour

JAMAICA TOUR

The Nueva Seville Spanish Church   1524–1534
The Seville Estate
St. Ann's Bay
St. Ann, Jamaica

This Gothic stone church was built on the order of the Spanish Abbott Peter Martyr to replace two wood and thatch churches destroyed by fire. The church was still incomplete when Seville Town was abandoned in 1534. It was described in 1688 by Hans Sloan, who said that it had three naves with rows of pillars and a very fine west gate.

Port Royal
Jamaica

Before Columbus's chance discovery of Jamaica, Port Royal existed as a large offshore fishing village for the Arawaks. In the 17th century, it became an ideal base for pirates, buccaneers, and merchants engaged in legal and illegal business. The population quickly grew to more than 8,000 in the 17th century, with in fine brick houses (some four stories high) with piped water, beer pubs, and a prison. Before long, Port Royal became one of the richest cities in the world, with a reputation for being one of the most wicked.

The earthquake of 1692 devastated the city, sinking two-thirds of it beneath the sea and killing 2,000 of its citizens. The British continued to use the remaining city as a naval station, but subsequent fires (1703) and hurricanes (1721, 1726, and 1744) never allowed it to regain its prominence. The 1952 hurricane left only 10 out of 260 modern buildings standing. The town was recently rebuilt, and archeological surveys are continuing to uncover relics from its turbulent past.

Louvered Screen Wall Around Verandah   1745
Seville Great House
Seville Estate
St. Ann's Bay
St. Ann, Jamaica

St. Peters Church   1725
Port Royal, Jamaica

St. Peters Church, the second oldest Anglican church on the island, was rebuilt in 1725 under the direction of Lewis Galdy after three previous churches had been destroyed by earthquake and fire.

Coke Chapel   1789
East Parade
Kingston, Jamaica

The Coke Chapel east of Parade replaced a smaller church known as Parade Chapel, which was founded in 1789 by Rev. Thomas Coke, a pioneer missionary.

Rodney Memorial
Spanish Town Square
Spanish Town, Jamaica

UWI Chapel
The University of the West Indies, Mona Campus
St. Andrew, Jamaica

Devon House   1881
Corner of Waterloo and Hope Road
Kingston, Jamaica

Devon House is the most elegant surviving 19-century mansion on the island. It was built in 1881 by George Steibel, a black shipwright's apprentice and builder's foreman, who sought and found his fortune in a Venezuelan gold mine. The Georgian-style architecture was adapted to tropical conditions, with wide louvered windows, deep patios, and wide overhangs. The former stables and carriage house were converted to The Grogge Shop and The Devonshire Restaurant, both open onto a courtyard shaded by a giant mango tree.

Harmony Hall   Late 1800s
On the St. Mary Coast near Ocho Rios
St. Ann, Jamaica

This Georgian building was constructed with timber walls, a shingle roof, and stone foundations.

Partners Merchant Bank   1890s
(Formerly Kingston Restoration Company Building)
3 Duke Street
Kingston, Jamaica

This is a two-story Georgian-style office building.

Craighton House   1805
Newcastle Road
St. Andrew, Jamaica

The original house, named after its first owner, George Craighton, was built in or around 1805. Located 2,600 feet above sea level, it is a very attractive colonial house with a large, flat plateau of lawn at the front and a commanding view to the east and west. The house served as a summer getaway from the heat for many notables at various times, including Sir John Peter Grant (governor around 1866), the Earl of Elgen, Sir Henry Blake (governor in 1880), and the Bishop of Kingston (at the beginning of the 20th century), who occupied the house for several months of the year. The house is currently owned by UCC, the largest coffee company in Japan, which operate in Jamaica as Jamaica UCC Blue Mountain Coffee Co. Ltd. This company bought Craighton House and Craighton Estate in 1981 and has reestablished the coffee crop there.

National Arena   1962
National Stadium Complex
Kingston, Jamaica

Norman Manley Law School
The University of the West Indies, Mona Campus
St. Andrew, Jamaica

Philip Sherlock Center for the Creative Arts
The University of the West Indies, Mona Campus
St. Andrew, Jamaica

OAHU TOUR

Meeting Hall
Island of New Zealand (Re-creation)
Polynesian Cultural Center
Laie, Oahu

Iolani Palace   1882
417 South King Street
Honolulu, Oahu

Filipino Dormitory   1919
Hawaii's Plantation Village
Waipahu, Oahu

Honolulu Hale   1929
Honolulu City Hall
Corner of King & Punchbowl Street
Honolulu, Oahu

Church of the Crossroads
1212 University Avenue
Honolulu, Oahu

USS Arizona War Memorial   1962
Ford Island
Pearl Harbor, Oahu

House
Diamond Head Road
Diamond Head, Oahu

This house has a Hawaiian tile roof.

House
3207 Diamond Head Road
Diamond Head, Oahu

This house has Spanish influences with a modern twist.

House
2506 Makiki Heights Drive
Makiki, Oahu

Commercial/Residential Tower
Waikiki Beach
Waikiki, Oahu

AUSTRALIA TOUR

The New Convention Center
Darling Harbor, Sydney
Photographer: Lee Askew III, FAIA

The Power Plant and Children's Museum
Sydney
Photographer: Lee Askew III, FAIA

Apartments
Kings Cross, Sydney
Photographer: Lee Askew III, FAIA

Condominium
Sydney
Photographer: Lee Askew III, FAIA

The Penthouse Condominium
Wooloomooloo
Photographer: Lee Askew III, FAIA

SOUTHERN CALIFORNIA TOUR

Pinney House
1355 Carroll Avenue
Westwood, California

Craftsman House
Corner of 36th Street and Arlington Avenue
Los Angeles, California

Holmey Hall   1929
Westside of Westwood Boulevard
Between Weyburn and LeConte Avenues
Westwood, California

Holiday House Motel   1950
(Richard J. Neutra
**   Dion Neutra–1954)**
27400 Pacific Coast Highway
Malibu, California

Elkay Apartments   1948
(Richard J. Neutra)
638–642 Kelton Avenue
Malibu, California

Tischer House   1949
(R.M. Schindler)
175 Greenfield Avenue
Westwood, California

APPENDIX **C**

Tables

TABLE 1 Classification of Scales

1. Types of structure	A. Cobwork, adobe, rural and ordinary stone buildings
	B. Brick, concrete block, half timber, bonded stonework
	C. Reinforced concrete and strong wooden buildings
2. Percentage of building damage	Q (a few)—above 5 percent
	N (many)—above 50 percent
	P (most)—75 percent or more
3. Classification	Grade 1. Slightly damaged, cracking, fall of damage from debris and plaster
	Grade 2. Moderate damage, cracking of walls, fall of roof tiles, cracking and fall of parts of chimneys.
	Grade 3. Heavy damage: large, deep cracks in walls, fall of chimneys
	Grade 4. Destruction: gaps in walls, partial collapse of buildings, internal and infill walls collapse
	Grade 5. Total damage: total collapse of buildings

TABLE 2 Effect on Buildings Based on the Classification of Scales

Intensity	Type A Q, N, P	Type B Q, N, P	Type C Q, N, P
VI—Strong	2, 1	1	
VII—Very strong	4, 3	2	
VIII—Destructive	5, 4	4, 3	3, 2
IX—Partially annihilating	5	5, 4	4, 3
X—Annihilating	5	5	5, 4

Source: Konya, Allan, *Design Primer for Hot Climates* Copyright 1980. Used with permission from Butterworths.

TABLE 3 Recommended Schedule for Nailing the Framing and Sheathing of a Well-Constructed Wood-Frame House

		Nails		
Joining	Nailing method	No.	Size	Placements
Joist header to joist	Endnail	3	16d	
Joist to sill or girder	Toenail	3	8d	
Header and edge joist to sill	Toenail		8d	16 in. (40 cm) on center
Bridging to joist	Toenail each end	2	8d	
Ledger strip to beam, 2 in. thick		3	16d	At each joist
Subfloor, boards				
1 × 6 in. and smaller		2	8d	To each joist
1 × 8 in.		3	8d	To each joist
Subfloor, plywood				
At edges			8d	6 in. (15 cm) on center
At intermediate joists			8d	8 in. (20 cm) on center
Subfloor (2 × 6, tongue and groove) to joist or girder	Blind nail (casing) and facenail	2	16d	
Sole plate to stud, horizontal assembly	Facenail	2	16d	At each stud
Top plate to stud, horizontal assembly	Endnail	2	16d	At each stud
Top plate to stud	Endnail	2	16d	
Stud to sole plate	Toenail	4	8d	
Sole plate to joist or blocking	Facenail		16d	16 in. (40 cm) on center
Double studs	Facenail, stagger		10d	16 in. (40 cm) on center
End stud of intersecting wall to exterior wall stud	Facenail		10d	16 in. (40 cm) on center
Upper top plate to lower top plate	Facenail		16d	16 in. (40 cm) on center
Upper top plate, laps and intersections	Facenail	2	16d	
Continuous header, two piece, each edge			12d	12 in. (30 cm) on center
Ceiling joist to top wall plates	Toenail	3	8d	
Ceiling joist laps at partition	Toenail	4	16d	

continued

209

TABLE 3 Recommended Schedule for Nailing the Framing and Sheathing of a Well-Constructed Wood-Frame House (*Continued*)

Joining	Nailing method	Nails		
		No.	Size	Placements
Rafters to top plate	Toenail	2	8d	
Rafters to ceiling joist	Facenail	3	10d	
Rafters to valley or hip rafter	Toenail	3	10d	
Ridge board to rafter	Endnail	3	10d	
Rafter to rafter through ridge board	Toenail	4	8d	
	Endnail	1	10d	
Collar beam to rafter				
2-in. member	Facenail	2	12d	
1-in. member	Facenail	3	8d	
1-in. diagonal let-in brace to each stud and plate (four nails at top)		2	8d	Placement
Built-up corner studs				
studs to blocking	Facenail	2	10d	Each side
intersecting stud to corner studs	Facenail		16d	12 in. (30 cm) on on center
Built-up girders and beams, 3 or more members	Facenail		20d	32 in. (80 cm) on center
Wall sheathing				
1 × 8 in. or less, horizontal	Facenail	2	8d	At each stud
1 × 6 in. or more, diagonal	Facenail	3	8d	At each stud
Wall sheathing, vertically applied plywood:				
⅜ in. and less thick	Facenail		6d	6 in. (15 cm) edge
½ in. and more thick	Facenail		8d	12 in. (30 cm) intermediate

Source: U.S. Forest Service, Research Paper FPL 33 "House Can Resist Hurricanes." Prepared by the U.S. Forest Service by L. O. Anderson and W. R. Smith (Madison, WI: Forest Laboratory, 1965).

TABLE 4   Maximum Ratio of Unsupported Height or Length to Nominal Thickness of Walls

Type of Masonry	Ratio
Solid masonry-bearing walls	20
Hollow unit masonry-bearing walls	18
Cavity walls	18*
Nonbearing walls	36[†]

*Thickness equal to the sum of the nominal thicknesses of the inner and outer widths.
[†]Based on the actual thickness of the partition, including plaster.
Source: American National Standard A41.1–1953 (R 1970).

Bibliography

JAMAICA

Black, Clinton (1961). *History of Jamaica* (Collins Press).

Cox, Oliver (1984). *Upgrading and Renewing the Historic City of Port Royal, Jamaica* (Shankland Cox, London).

Craham, Margaret E., and Knight, Franklin W. (1980). *Africa and the Caribbean, The Legacies of a Link* (John Hopkins University Press).

Crayton, Michael, and Walvin, James (1970). *A Jamaican Plantation* (University of Toronto Press).

Duly, Colin (1969). *The House of Mankind* (Thames & Hudson).

Harman, Carter, and the Editors of *Life* (1963). *The West Indies, Life World Library* (Time Incorporated.).

Hulme, Peter (1992). *Colonial Encounters, Europe and the Native Caribbean 1492–1797* (Routledge).

Hulme, Peter, and Whitehead, Neil L. (1992). *Wild Majesty: Encounters with Caribs from Columbus to the Present Day* (Clarendon Press).

Macpherson, John (1977). *Caribbean Lands* (Longman Group Ltd.).

Quarry, John (1957). *The West Indies: The Land and the People Series* (Macmillan).

Rogatz, Lowell J. (1928). *The Fall of the Planter Class in the British Caribbean* (Century).

Rogozinski, Jan (1994). *A Brief History of the Caribbean, From the Arawak and the Carib to the Present* (Meridian).

Roume de St. Laurent, P.R. (1777) A Report to Lord Macartney Governor of Grenada, of his visit to Trinidad. Public Record Office, State Papers Colonial C.O. 101/3.

Sancho de Alquiza to the King of Spain, 14th June 1612. British Museum, Additional Mss. 36320. Translated from Spanish.

Sheridan, Richard B. (1974). *Sugar and Slavery* (Johns Hopkins University Press).

Sherlock, Sir Phillip (1973). *West Indian Nation* (St. Martin's Press).

U.S. Weather Bureau (1980). *Weather Summary, West Indies* (U.S. Department of Commerce).

Waddell, D.A.G. (1967). *The West Indies and the Guianas* (Prentice-Hall).

HAWAII★

Bell, Roger (1947). *Last Among Equals: Hawaiian Statehood and American Politics."* (University of Hawaii Press).

Dickey, Charles W. & Jay, Robert (1992). *The Architecture of Charles W. Dickey, Hawaii and California*

Harris, Bill (1987). *Hawaii* (designed and produced by Ted Smart and David Gibbon).

Sandler, Rob (1993). *Architecture in Hawaii* (Mutual Publishing).

Storrs, Lee W. (1966). *The Islands* (Holt, Rinehart and Winston).

Tamura, Eileen H. (1994). *Americanization, Acculturation, and Ethnic Identity* (University of Illinois Press).

Tate, Merze (1968). *Hawaii—Reciprocity or Annexation?* (Michigan State University Press).

Webb, Nancy & Jean Francis (1956). *The Hawaiian Islands—From Monarchy to Democracy* (Viking Press).

Wise, Handy, Emory, Bryan, and Buck, (1965). *Ancient Hawaiian Civilization* (A Series of Lectures Delivered at the Kamehameha Schools). (C.E. Tuttle Co.)

AUSTRALIA

A History of Australia—From the Earliest Times to the Age of MacQuarie (1962). (Melbourne University Press and Cambridge University Press).

Australian Architects—Ken Woolley (1986). (published in Australia by Royal Australian Institute of Architects Education Division).

Australian Architects—Phillip Cox (1985). (Published in Australia by Royal Australian Institute of Architects, Education Division)

Baedeker (1995). *Australia* (Macmillan Travel).

Crawford, R.M. (1952). *Australia* (Hutchinson's University Library).

★ Excerpts from the section on "Plantation Architecture" (p. 44), including notes on Chinese and Japanese Influences (pp. 45 and 46), were taken from *Americanization, Acculturation, and Ethnic Identity: The Nisei Generation in Hawaii*. Copyright 1994 by the Board of Trustees of the University of Illinois. Used with the permission of the University of Illinois Press.

Elkin, A.P. (1964). *The Australian Aborigines* (Doubleday Anchor Book).

Grattan, Hartley C. (1947). *Australia* (University of California Press).

Griggs, Michael, and Paroissien, Leon (1983). *Old Continent, New Building—Contemporary Australian Architecture* (David Ell Press Pty. Ltd.).

Hughes, Robert (1986). *The Fatal Shore—The Epic of Australia's Founding*

Saini, Balwant, and Joyce, Ray (1982). *The Australian House—Homes of the Tropical North* (Lansdowne Press).

Ward, Russel (1965). *Australia* (Prentice-Hall).

SOUTHERN CALIFORNIA

Bael, Kurt (1958). Architecture of the California Missions, Berkeley: UC Press.

Banham, Reyner (1971). *Los Angeles, The Architecture of Four Ecologies* (Penguin Press).

Baxter, Sylvester (1901). *Spanish Colonial Architecture in Mexico* (Boston University Press).

Bruner, E.L. (1926). *California Type of Architecture* (A & E October, pp. 97–99).

Duell, Prentice (September 1921). "A Note on California Architecture" (*California Southland*).

Gebhard, David (May 1967). "The Spanish Colonial Revival in Southern California" (*Society of Architectural Historians Journal*, pp. 31–47).

Gebhard, David (1971). *Schindler* (Viking Press).

Gleye, Paul (1981). *The Architecture of Los Angeles* (Rosebud Books).

Grey, Elmer (January 1905). "Architecture in Southern California" (*Architectural Record*, pp. 1–17).

Hannaford, Donald R. (1931). *Spanish Colonial or Adobe Architecture in California, 1800–1850* (Architecture Book Publishing Co.).

Kirker, Harold (1960). *California's Architectural Frontier—Peregrine Smith*.

Lummis, Charles F. (1895). "Something about the Adobe" (*Land of Sunshine*, pp. 48–50).

Lummis, Charles F. (April 1898). "The Old Missions" (*Land of Sunshine*, pp. 247–53).

McWilliams, Carey (1979). *Southern California* (Peregrine Smith, Inc.).

Mooney, Mary E. (1900). *Side-lights on Old Los Angeles* (Historic Society of Southern California).

Neutra, Richard (1935). *The New Building in California* (Arts and Architecture).

Starr, Kevin (1990). *Material Dreams—Southern California Through the 1920's* (Oxford University Press).

Starr, Kevin (1985). *Inventing the Dream—California Through the Progressive Era* (Oxford University Press).

Starr, Kevin (1973). *Americans and the California Dream, 1850–1915* (Oxford University Press).

FURTHER READING—GENERAL

Dubin, and Long, (1978). *Energy Conservation Standards—for Building Design, Construction and Operations* (McGraw-Hill).

Jarmul, Seymore (1980). *The Architect's Guide to Energy Conservation—Realistic Energy Planning for Buildings* (McGraw-Hill).

Konya, Allan (1980). *Design Primer for Hot Climates* (Whitney Library of Design, Architectural Press).

Neuman (1993) "Tropical Cyclone" (The Southwest Indian Ocean).

Olgyay, Victor, (1963) "Design with Climate, Princeton Univ. Press, Princeton, NJ. ( ).

Pilkey, Neal (1983). *Coastal Design* (Van Nostrand Reinhold Company).

Watson, Donald, and Labs, Kenneth (1983). *Climatic Design—Energy Efficient Building Principles and Practice* (McGraw-Hill).

Winter, Stern Associates Inc. *The Passive Solar Construction Handbook* (Rodale Books).

Wright, David (1978). *Natural Solar Architecture—A Passive Primer* (Van Nostrand Reinhold).

Index